CONTENTS

За пријава на престојувалиште - пријава и одјава
на живеалиште односно пријава на промена на стан
du bulletin de déclaration dé séjour - déclaration dé séjour et annonce de
depart ou déclaration de changement de demeure

Презиме и име- Nom et prénom

Ден месец и година на раѓањето - Jour, mois et année de naissance

Место и држава на раѓањето - Place ... ie naissance

Вид и бр ... идентитет
Espéce et n ... ente

Пријавил престо... јавил живеалиште
Décla ...

Датум на пријавата   Датум на одјавата
Date de déclaration de séjour   te de l'annonce le depart

Образец бр 11
на 2861 - 90

(A

на овластеното лице)
l'employe autorise

Photograph of Frank Cottrell Boyce attached to his Macedonian visa.

Michael Winterbottom

WELCOME TO SARAJEVO

WELCOME TO SARAJEVO
Frank Cottrell Boyce

Based on the book, *Natasha's Story*,
by Michael Nicholson

faber and faber

First published in 1997
by Faber and Faber Limited
3 Queen Square London WCIN 3AU

Photoset by Parker Typesetting Service Ltd, Leicester
Printed in England by Clays Ltd, St Ives plc

A CIP record for this book
is available from the British Library

ISBN 0–571–19385–4

2 4 6 8 10 9 7 5 3 1

INTRODUCTION

Opposite the block of flats in which I was born, there was a vast meadow of rubble which had been made, twenty years earlier, by a bomb dropped during the May Blitz. I grew up with the feeling I had missed the Big Event. The War was over, and there would never be another one. Not in Europe. I pestered my parents for tales of evacuation and air raids. I built squadrons of Airfix Spitfires. I never went anywhere without my arms stretched out like wings, making engine noises. If there was a war, I would be ready for it. Then a war did start in Europe and somehow I barely noticed. I was busy raising children, making a living, watching the O.J. Simpson trial. I knew people who were interested – a man from our parish collected a Luton van full of tinned food and drove it to Vukovar himself; an ex-boyfriend of my sister went to Croatia to take photographs. But when Graham Broadbent asked me if I wanted to write a film about Sarajevo, I said yes because I needed the money and because I wanted to work with Michael Winterbottom again, not because I had any strong feelings about it.

I began by watching tapes. I saw the amazing films made by SAGA in Sarajevo during the siege, films like *I Burned Legs*, *MGM – Sarajevo* and *Bums and Dogs*. I watched Martin Bell's *Forcing the Peace*, and Michael Nicholson's passionate reports from the Ljubica Ivezic orphanage. Scenes of horror and heroism unfolded across the screen – lines of refugees, people queuing for water under sniper fire. Why had I been so apathetic about this? How had I allowed it to slip by me? Then I saw a tape by John Sweeney about the killing of a British photographer in Croatia. When they showed his face I reached for the freeze frame. That was him. Paul Jenks. My sister's ex. He was dead and I didn't even know. I rang my sister and she hadn't known either. It was then that the invisibility of the war really came home to me.

I'm not a journalist. I wasn't in Sarajevo during the siege. There were lots of things I didn't know. But I did know this one big fact – that this war had been ignored. I knew because I had ignored it.

Nothing I knew about screenwriting was any use to me when I

vii

was working on *Welcome to Sarajevo*.

Graham had bought the rights to Michael Nicholson's book *Natasha's Story* – an account of how Nicholson had met and finally adopted an orphan girl in Sarajevo during the siege. To begin with, this bothered me. I had seen enough films about Western journalists in faraway wars, struggling with their consciences and bosses while nameless natives got napalmed somewhere up country. When I read the book I felt differently. Nicholson had rescued one child. It was an act of moral heroism – a human gesture in an inhuman situation – but it wasn't epic. He was not Gladys Aylward, leading hundreds of children through enemy territory in *The Inn of the Sixth Happiness*. He had not unmasked a CIA conspiracy or smuggled secrets. It was moving and admirable, but also very simple. I could tell this story and still have room for other stories. I could use Nicholson as a starting point, then open out and tell the story of the siege itself – the daily grind of collecting firewood, scoring tobacco, wishing for soap, longing for something to happen. I could write a script that had some of the power of the SAGA films but was also accessible to a wider audience. The Nicholson character would be an Everyman, guiding us through the city. He would be based not on Nicholson himself but on Anybody. I wouldn't even go and meet Nicholson. It sounded really convincing when I pitched it and I got the job.

I thought it would be easy. I had a thousand great stories. Stories about how the people of Sarajevo had tried heroically to keep their city functioning and civilized while being pounded by two million Serb shells. There was the Sarajevo FC Football team, whose pitch became a mass grave; the Miss Sarajevo contest; the 'Beyond the End of the World' film festival held in the Radnik cinema on Snipers' Alley, when people ran a gauntlet of gunfire to get to the movies and so on. There was no shortage of heroes. There was Youssef Hajir – a refugee from Syria who opened the trauma hospital in Dobrinja in July 1992 and never lost a single patient to infection. There was Vedran Smiljovic who organized musicians everywhere to play Albinoni's *Adagio for Strings* at midday on the day the UN Council of Ministers came to visit. And of course there was Mrs Zoric, the Serb woman who ran the Ljubica Ivezic orphanage within sight of the Serb artillery, and who appears in the film as Mrs Savic.

I thought it would be easy because I had never written an Everyman character. Everyman characters are a swine. If Nicholson was to be the lens through which we looked at Sarajevo, then he had to be transparent. I'd spent years learning to push and explore characters. Now I had to write one that you would barely notice. All the interesting questions about Nicholson – like what made him pick Natasha, what his wife and other children thought of it, and so on – had to be closed down. It wasn't enough not to raise them; I had to make sure the audience didn't raise them either. They had to feel that it was the least he could have done, that they would have done the same. Henderson had to be a character with no 'character arc'. He had to go to Sarajevo, do his thing, and then carry on. In these times, when every adventure is played as therapy ('Yes, I did save the World from invading aliens, but more importantly, I discovered some important truths about my relationship with my father') the idea of a man just taking things in his stride was a kind of movie heresy.

The second problem was structure. Everyone is an expert in movie structure now. Everyone knows that films have three acts and that all the art is in the subtlety of the set-up and the aptness of the pay-off. However, Michael Winterbottom and I agreed that the film would only get the urgency it needed if we stuck as closely as possible to the facts. But facts are not like drama. In drama, characters make decisions, create their own fate and live with the consequences. In life, things happen by coincidence and chance. People set things up that don't pay off. They find themselves in the middle of situations before the exposition. Important characters vanish unexpectedly from their lives. Business is left unfinished and we are somehow never quite on stage for the big finale.

I tried at first to get the story into the traditional form, to put Henderson in control. I had him meeting Emira in the street more or less at the opening of the film. I made him seek her out. I made it harder for him to get Emira out of Sarajevo. But it took up too much space and it wasn't true. The fact is that Nicholson just happened to bump into someone who could help him one night in the Holiday Inn.

So I went the other way. I tried to write a screenplay in which the sequence seemed as random as war, in which the audience would never be quite sure where the next scene was coming from. I deliberately left Henderson's first meeting with Emira as late as I could. I put other children – the altar boy, the girl in the hospital – in the film to show that there was nothing special about Emira. I tried to get in as many scenes without Henderson as possible. I followed minor characters back to their homes. I had a five-minute section in the middle of the film about Arkan, the leading exponent of Ethnic Cleansing, in which none of our characters appeared. I added a section about the discovery of the concentration camps at Manjaca and Omarska. I didn't feel this should be sensationalized or could be re-created, so I just pasted it in as a fact and suggested we use the original ITN footage. I read what I had written and realized that it wasn't a script, but a collage. I tried to get away with it by putting in 'chapter headings' to guide the reader through it. But it was a mess.

I had a crisis of faith in the whole thing. Every film I watched seemed infinitely better. I watched Zinnemann's *The Search*, in which Montgomery Clift adopts a refugee child and tries to form a relationship with him. It was so moving that I started a rewrite set entirely in Surrey which concentrated on Emira's inability to adjust to peace. Graham heard about this and managed to talk me down. I watched *Under Fire* and wanted to put in helicopters and elephants. I watched *The Killing Fields* and realized that Bruce Robinson had already done it all.

Michael, however, liked the mess. He believed he could make a film that worked not by linear narrative momentum, but by the immediacy of the action itself. He took what I did and pushed it further. He removed the helpful chapter headings. Taking his cue from the concentration camp suggestion, he peppered the film with real footage. To their credit, David Aukin and Allon Reich at Channel Four understood and supported what we were trying to do. I was expecting script doctor notes about Henderson's character bypass and the late introduction of the main story, but they never came.

It was harder to persuade people that the only place the film could be shot was Sarajevo itself. There were problems with insurance, and with landmines. Once he got there, Michael's obsession with getting as close as possible to what really happened led to more rewrites. He made me take out a wonderful joke about the Sarajevo football team because it wasn't quite true. I had a section about the infamous tragedy of Bosko and Admira which he made me rewrite because I had written it for daytime and it actually happened at night. The fact that the script was so fragmentary meant that it never really locked into shape the way a more linear film would. Right through the shoot, I was adding and taking away. I ended up dropping the Arkan section and the 'chapter' about Bosko and Admira. It was a question of balance, of how long we could leave the main story parked up, how far from it we could stray.

By now I was obsessed with the war. Every time I was asked for a little bit of extra dialogue, I would send an entire new draft encompassing all the latest developments at Dayton. One day in Skopje, Michael asked me for two pages and I wrote twenty-two. He shrugged a Michael shrug, said, 'Good. Thanks,' then went and patiently excavated what he needed. I got much of this new material from Michael Nicholson. I still hadn't met him, but he was generous with his faxes.

By the time we got to post-production we felt more confident and moved material around that we had tried to keep in chronological order in the script. For instance, in the script I had made a big palaver out of the convoy's attempt to leave the city. There were ticking clocks and snipers' sights, the whole bit. Then later in the film, I went through hoops trying to wedge in the news that in a second convoy some babies had been shot. In post-production, it became obvious that if we put the second convoy first, it would create lots of tension for the convoy on which Emira and Henderson were travelling and it would save me a lot of embarrassing exposition later on.

But the script never felt finished. When we finally screened it for Miramax, I buttonholed Michael in the loo and outlined a new opening. 'It's too late, Frank.' Michael Nicholson turned up, so we did meet in the end. We didn't talk about Sarajevo, only about Natasha. She's a keen tennis player now, an aspiring professional. 'Great,' I said. 'Can't wait to hear what you think of the film.' In fact, I sneaked out before the end.

When I started to write *Welcome to Sarajevo*, the war in Bosnia was still raging. For all I knew it might go on for four more years. I wanted to make a film that would make it impossible for people to go on ignoring it. In the end, we were too late. Thank God. But although the siege is over, the peace has not begun. If the film makes people spend ninety minutes thinking about Bosnia during this uneasy time, then it's done its job.

Frank Cottrell Boyce

1997

Welcome to Sarajevo was first shown as part of the Official Competition at the 1997 Cannes Film Festival. The cast and crew includes:

HENDERSON	Stephen Dillane
FLYNN	Woody Harrelson
NINA	Marisa Tomei
EMIRA	Emira Nusevic
JANE CARSON	Kerry Fox
RISTO	Goran Visnjic
GREG	James Nesbitt
ANNIE MCGEE	Emily Lloyd
JACKET	Igor Dzambazov
MRS SAVIC	Gordana Gadzic

Casting:	Simone Ireland & Vanessa Pereira
Costume Designer:	Janty Yates
Production Designer:	Mark Geraghty
Director of Photography:	Daf Hobson
Editor:	Trevor Waite
Original Music:	Adrian Johnston
Screenplay:	Frank Cottrell Boyce
	based on the book, *Natasha's Story*,
	by Michael Nicholson
Produced by	Graham Broadbent and
	Damian Jones
Directed by	Michael Winterbottom

A Dragon Pictures production

A Channel Four Films and Miramax Films presentation

VLADIMIR I can't go on like this.
ESTRAGON That's what you think.
                    Waiting for Godot

1   A Wedding

STOCK FOOTAGE. PRE-TITLE.

Open with the epic image – the Fall of Vukovar. A sizeable city reduced to a pile of rubble. Streams of refugees pour out of the rubble. Old people and children trudge forward, weeping, carrying little bundles. Behind them, a pall of smoke rises into the sky. It looks like something from World War Two. But then a subtitle appears.

VUKOVAR, NOVEMBER 11TH 1991

EXT. BOMBED OUT STREETS, VUKOVAR. DAY.

Michael Henderson appears in the front of shot, talking directly to camera. He is a veteran war correspondent and this is his report.

> ### HENDERSON
> Today the city of Vukovar has fallen. It is now no more than a heap of rubble. In the past two months, the Serbs have pounded it with more than two *million* shells. These survivors are heading for Bosnia, hoping to escape the war. But tonight we must face the possibility that what we have seen here is only the beginning.
>
> CUT TO:

STOCK FOOTAGE. MONTAGE.

Jolly, upbeat advertisements for the Winter Olympics in Sarajevo dance across the screen.

SARAJEVO

INT. BEAUTY SALON, SARAJEVO. DAY.

MAY 1992

A cheap transistor radio plays an ecstatically upbeat pop song. Two girls – a young bride, and her fourteen-year-old sister – are sitting under hair-driers, their heads crowned in curlers. They nod their heads in time to the music, making their curlers wobble.

They are being attended by a young hairdresser. Slouched on a deep chair in the corner, is the bride's mother.

Suddenly, the radio stops, and the hair-driers sigh and then rattle into silence. Everyone – except the mother – shrieks with panic. Resignedly, the mother hauls herself onto her feet, she asks the hairdresser a question. The hairdresser replies and the mother shuffles through the shop.

INT. REAR OF BEAUTY SALON, SARAJEVO. DAY.

We follow the mother through to the back of the shop. She looks down at a rusty generator. Thinks, makes the sign of the cross, yanks a set of rosary beads up from her belt, kisses them, then lands the generator a hefty, well-aimed kick with her boot.

INT. BEAUTY SALON, SARAJEVO. DAY.

In the shop, the radio sings back into life. The bride beams ecstatically.

CUT TO:

INT. FLAT, SARAJEVO. DAY.

The sister is struggling into a satiny bridesmaid's dress. Her head appears, still crowned with rollers.

The bride's veil is put on.

CUT TO:

4

INT. CHURCH, SARAJEVO. DAY.

An Altar Boy hurries into the sacristy of the church, where a priest tells him to hurry up.

    CUT TO:

EXT. FLAT, SARAJEVO. DAY.

The bride, sister and mother emerge from the flats into the street. All around is dereliction. There is a wrecked car at the side of the road. The bride pulls on the skirt of her gown and starts to walk. Some boys shout remarks at her Sister, who is embarrassed and pleased.

INT. CHURCH, SARAJEVO. DAY.

In the sacristy, the Altar Boy lights the thurable. He blows on a block of charcoal, making it glow, spoons on a little incense, lets the brass lid fall shut.

EXT. CHURCH, SARAJEVO. DAY.

The bridal party nears the church. The bride pauses to adjust her veil. Suddenly, the mother reels backwards into the rubble, almost dragging the others down with her.

The music on the soundtrack stops. The first 'real sound' we hear is the piercing, animal scream of the bride as she looks down at her mother. The older woman is lying on the floor, surrounded by her blood and shuddering convulsively. She has been shot. The bride goes to help her mother.

Immediately a shot rings out and a column of dust spirals into the air. The bride shrinks back in fright. Then there is another shot and the mother is dead.

    CUT TO:

EXT. CHURCH, SARAJEVO. DAY.

We are watching news footage. A long shot of the mother, still lying in the middle of the road. The priest is bending over the body, administering the last rites but no one else is near. On Voice Over, we hear Michael Henderson – an English television war correspondent – piecing together information.

HENDERSON
(*voice-over*)
Woman in her sixties . . . shot by sniper fire. The bride's mother. I think she's the bride's mother . . .

EXT. CHURCH, SARAJEVO. DAY.

The English voice blends first into Italian, then Spanish, then French, American and German as we pull out to find a line of cameramen and journalists photographing the scene. Henderson is at the end of the line. With him is the cameraman, Greg.

HENDERSON
(*to Greg*)
Get the cross on top of the church. I think the family must be Croatian.

Greg's camera picks up on two young men, wrenching the bonnet off the wrecked car. Using this as a shield, they make their way over to the corpse. Henderson's eye is drawn to the Altar Boy, who is standing directly opposite him on the other side of the street. The Altar Boy is shouting and gesticulating straight at Henderson. Henderson is unsettled by this.

HENDERSON
Greg . . . that altar boy.

GREG
What? Oh. Got him.

Greg has the Altar Boy in his sights now. The boy still seems to be talking straight at them. He now points at Henderson.

HENDERSON
What does he want?

Suddenly, the Altar boy flinches and everyone else screams. The sniper has reappeared on the roof of the building opposite. His gun is clearly visible. All the cameramen and journalists hit the floor. Then, working on instinct, start pointing their cameras towards the sniper, from behind whatever cover is possible.

Yes! Got the sniper!

Across the road, the Altar Boy is the first to rise to his feet. He looks straight at Henderson, holds out both arms and starts to shout again.

HENDERSON
OK. That's enough.

GREG
Hang on, hang on . . .

Henderson looks across the road. There is now no sign of the Altar Boy.

HENDERSON
He's gone.

Down the line of journalists, we pick up on an American journalist, named Flynn. He stands up and walks – erect and unhurried – to the side of the priest and helps him load the body onto the car bonnet. All the other journalists start shooting this dramatic incident, including Greg.

Let's go.

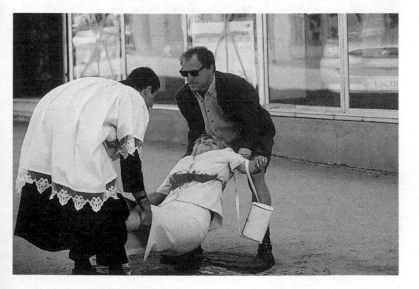

GREG

You don't want this?

Henderson is already walking away. Greg catches up with him.

CUT TO:

EXT. STREETS, SARAJEVO. DAY.

Henderson and Greg are going back to their car. They jog down a bombed-out alley. They stop, looking bewildered.

HENDERSON

Where's the van?

GREG

Shit.

The silence is eerie. They are painfully aware of empty windows looking down at them.

Let's go back.

HENDERSON

No. Wait. Through here.

He points to a wall that has been shattered by bombing. Henderson leads Greg through the bombed remains of somebody's living room. Shattered bric-à-brac all over the floor.

GREG

Are you sure?

HENDERSON

No.

Something moves in the rubble. They both spin round. A rat.

EXT. STREETS, SARAJEVO. DAY.

They climb over the masonry into the next street and look up at the windows. All blank. There could be a sniper in any one of them.

GREG

Where is he?

8

There is a shout from further up the street. Instinctively, Henderson and Greg duck down behind the wall. A little girl runs down the street, passing just in front of them, pushing a child's pram full of firewood.

Henderson and Greg stand up and climb over the wall into the street. They dash across to the far wall and then start to hurry down the street in the shadow of the wall.

This is the wrong street.

HENDERSON
No it's not. Just keep moving.

GREG
Shit.

They come to the corner at the bottom of the street. They hesitate. Suddenly, someone steps out in front of them, and starts shouting at them in Croat. It is the Altar Boy. What he is saying seems urgent. Is he angry or is it some kind of warning? Henderson and Greg want to move on but feel they can't just walk past the boy. They look anxiously back the way they came. It's a tense, disorientating moment.

Jesus.

HENDERSON
Where's the bloody van?

There is a sudden squeal of brakes and they both spin round to see a camper van powering down the road towards them. It slides to a halt in front of them.

JOEY
They put road-blocks. Looking for the sniper. I turn the van round. Others are going to be stuck here for hours.

They start to get in the van. The Altar Boy keeps shouting.

GREG
Can you tell us what he wants?

Joey looks uncomfortable.

JOEY
In English?

HENDERSON

No. In Old Icelandic.

GREG

Does he need help?

JOEY

Yes. Of course.

HENDERSON

Can we get out of here before we're shot?

Henderson gets into the van and starts to scribble notes. Greg hesitates before getting in. He finds a piece of chocolate in his pocket and hands it to the Altar Boy. The boy lets it drop but stares steadily at the van as it starts up and begins to move off.

INT. CAR. STREETS, SARAJEVO. DAY.

Suddenly, there is the snap of a rifle shot. A bullet has caught the windscreen of the van, nicking a hole in the glass, but not shattering the shield.

GREG

What was that?

Joey winds down the window and starts to shout in Serbo-Croat and to wave his fist. He turns briefly to Henderson.

JOEY

Snipers. Cheeky bastards. This is my own street. I live just down there. Bastards.

He starts to yell out of the window again. There are answering yells from inside the buildings and doorways. Henderson curses. Greg slides down in his seat.

HENDERSON

Could we get out of here, do you think?

JOEY

Sure. Any minute. No one is going to scare me out of my own neighbourhood . . .

But instead of driving off, Joey opens the door of the car, steps out to yell

*even louder and gesticulate more wildly. As soon as his foot touches the
floor, there is another shot. Joey jumps back into the car, slams the door
shut after him and starts to drive like a maniac.*

INT. CORRIDOR, TV CENTRE, SARAJEVO. EVENING.

The place has an ad hoc *feeling. It's heaving with journalists.
Henderson and Greg rush through to the edit room.*

INT. EDIT SUITE, TV STATION. EVENING.

Henderson and Greg entering the ad hoc *edit suite. They are met by
Jane Carson. She is neat and competent. Henderson is brisk with her.*

> HENDERSON
>
> We need a new driver.

> JANE
>
> What? Do you know how long it took me to find Joey? He
> used to be a cabbie. He knows this city and he speaks . . .

> HENDERSON
>
> He's an idiot.

> GREG
>
> He's been selling our petrol. He's also an idiot.

> HENDERSON
>
> When we got back today, Joey wasn't there. We could've
> been killed. Is that true, about the petrol?

> GREG
>
> It was full this morning and it's almost empty now.

> JANE
>
> Shit.

CUT TO:

INT. EDIT ROOM. EVENING.

*Greg and Henderson are sitting in front of a little video monitor, going
through their report. They are looking at the footage of the Altar Boy.
He suddenly flinches in response to something off-screen. The picture cuts*

to a great shot of the sniper on the roof. Greg and Henderson keep muttering self-congratulations.

GREG

Brilliant.

JANE

I've just seen this amazing footage of Flynn under fire.
                    (*No response.*)
Have we got any of that?

Henderson and Greg continue to be extravagantly absorbed by the images on the screen. They don't look at Jane.

HENDERSON

No. No we haven't.

JANE
                    (*rattled*)
Why's that?

HENDERSON

Why's what?

JANE

Why has everyone else got this amazing footage but not us?

HENDERSON

Well personally, I blame a general decline in journalistic standards; what about you, Greg?

GREG

It's all that news-is-entertainment bollocks isn't it. So patronizing. I hate that.

HENDERSON

Yeah I hate that too. What about you, Jane?

JANE

I think he did something brave and the viewer will always respond to bravery.

CUT TO:

INT. HOLIDAY INN. EVENING.

Pick up on Flynn's report playing on a big TV monitor. It looks epic. A crowd of journalists is watching. They all start to cheer. Flynn stands up and takes the applause.

FLYNN
No, no. No applause. Please. Cash only.

Henderson and Greg are watching this at some remove. Henderson is practically snarling. He goes to leave when Flynn spots him.

Henderson. Michael Henderson.

He shoves his way through the crowd, to Henderson, carrying a bottle of whiskey and a pair of tumblers. He offers Henderson his free hand.

I saw your report from Vukovar.

HENDERSON
Really?

FLYNN
You drink whiskey, don't you? I have a case, a case of whiskey. Here.

He hands over the whiskey. Henderson takes a sip.

I loved that report. That was a great report. The Vukovar one.

HENDERSON
Thank you.

FLYNN
No. I mean it. It was a great report. I really liked it. You were at the wedding today, weren't you?

HENDERSON
Yes. Yes I was.
(*beat*)
And I really honestly and sincerely admire your . . . whiskey. It's great whiskey. Really.

FLYNN
Thank you. It means a lot.

Henderson smiles and goes. Flynn knows he has been got at.

CUT TO:

INT. CORRIDOR, HOLIDAY INN. EVENING.

Greg and Henderson are walking down a corridor, towards their bedrooms.

GREG
It's not Flynn's fault. He was just trying to help.

HENDERSON
We're not here to help. We're here to report.

GREG
Oh right. Course.

Greg turns to open the door to his bedroom. Henderson heads off down the corridor.

Michael . . .

Henderson turns to look at him.

Are you OK?

HENDERSON
What d'you mean?

There is an implicit challenge in Henderson's response.

GREG
Nothing. I just . . . wondered. Good night.

He goes into his room.

CUT TO:

INT. BALLROOM, HOLIDAY INN. NIGHT.

Flynn is having a drink with Jane and another Englishwoman, Annie McGee.

FLYNN
This is great whiskey. Mr Henderson said so and he should know.

JANE

Don't let him get to you.

He scars the side of the bottle with a diamond pinkie ring.

FLYNN

We'll drink up to the line. Always make all the important decisions before you start drinking.

JANE

I liked your report. I liked what you did. It was brave.

ANNIE

I thought it stank.

FLYNN

Oh you thought it stank? Is that right?

ANNIE

It wasn't about the siege. It was about you. It was . . . lightweight.

FLYNN

Lightweight? Me? Lightweight? You are kidding. Do you know where I'm going next week? I am going to Romania. To that city they have there. What's it called?

JANE

Bucharest.

FLYNN

Bucharest. I'm going to Bucharest to cover a Michael Jackson. Now would they send a lightweight to cover a story like that? A Michael Jackson concert. Jane, come with me. I love you.

JANE

Is this whiskey going with you?

FLYNN

Maybe.

JANE

I'll come.

16

CUT TO:

INT. HENDERSON'S ROOM, HOLIDAY INN. NIGHT.

INT. BEDROOM, HENDERSON'S HOUSE, ENGLAND. NIGHT.

Henderson has just made a phone call. He gets through. He is calling his wife, Helen.

                    HELEN
Hello.

                    HENDERSON
Helen? It's me . . .

An answering machine kicks in, with Helen's voice on the recorded message.

                    HELEN
                    (*live*)
Oh. I'm sorry. The answerphone.

                    HENDERSON
It's OK.

He holds the phone away from his ear just in time to avoid getting blasted by the ear-splitting tone.

                    HELEN
I'm sorry. I put it on while I was putting the kids to bed. I must have fallen asleep.

                    HENDERSON
Are you OK?

                    HELEN
Fine. What time is it?

                    HENDERSON
We're two hours ahead so . . .

                    HELEN
Oh God . . . she's awake again. Can you hear that?

He can hear a little girl shouting, Mummy!

17

HENDERSON
Yeah. You go. I just . . . I'm all right.

HELEN
(shouting)
I'm coming!

(to Henderson)
I'd better go.

HENDERSON
I know. I just said that. What's she saying?

HELEN
She's asking for that bloody doll again. The one that went missing. You don't know where it is do you? Look, I've got to go.

HENDERSON
Good-night.

For a moment, the child's voice comes blasting through the phone before the line goes dead. Henderson replaces the phone and suddenly the whole hotel rocks.

CUT TO:

INT. CORRIDOR, HOLIDAY INN. NIGHT.

There are faces looking out of bedroom doors right the way down the corridor. The hotel has been hit by a shell. There is lots of discussion going on. We pick up lines like: 'They're shelling us.' 'It's just a stray.' 'You should put your mattress up against the window.' 'It's safer to sleep in the corridor, I think. No glass.'

Pick up on Greg dashing out of his room with his camera.

CUT TO:

INT. HENDERSON'S ROOM, HOLIDAY INN. NIGHT.

Henderson is jamming his mattress up against the windows. Then he notices another sound. Laughter. Childish laughter. He crosses gingerly to the window and looks out. He looks down.

EXT. STREETS/HOLIDAY INN. NIGHT.

There on the street below, alone and still wearing his surplice, is the Altar Boy. As Henderson looks, the boy lifts his head slowly, deliberately and stares straight into Henderson's eyes.

    CUT TO:

EXT. SARAJEVO. NIGHT.

The city illuminated and then plunged into darkness by flashes of shell fire.

Greg is up on the roof, shooting this. Occasionally giving little whoops of triumph and joy. The shelling thunders on.

    CUT TO:

2   Risto's Jacket

EXT. FLATS, SARAJEVO. MORNING.

People are queueing for water in the basement of a block of run-down flats. One of the people is a young man with a tartan shopping trolley loaded with empty plastic bottles. He comes to the front of the queue and starts to fill the bottles. His name is Risto.

    CUT TO:

EXT. DOORWAY, FLATS, SARAJEVO. MORNING.

Pick up Risto waiting in the doorway of the flats. There is a BEWARE SNIPERS *sign opposite the doorway. The young man waits. An older man is standing in the doorway, keeping watch. He signals to Risto and, on the command, Risto hurries off across the waste ground, dragging the trolley behind him.*

    CUT TO:

INT. RISTO'S FLAT. MORNING.

Risto pouring water into a pan on top of a twig-burning stove. He takes out his wallet and carefully unwraps a razor blade, ready to shave.

CUT TO:

INT. ASHA'S PUB. MORNING.

A group of young, bright, Bohemian people. One of them is wearing a beautiful red jacket. He is called Jacket. Another is a good-looking young student named Bosko. Later in the film he will die a hideous death but for now he is admiring some Barbie Dolls which Jacket has put on the table. These are dressed in the costumes of various militias and ethnicities. Jacket is going through them. The conversation is in Bosnian.

JACKET
(*Bosnian*)

This is Croat Barbie. Over here we have Serb Barbie. These look like breasts but they're really artillery. Amputee Barbie. Head-Blown-Off Barbie. Got them all.

They look up and see Risto arriving. They all shout his name as he arrives. He joins them. Bosko feels Risto's cheek.

BOSKO

(*Bosnian*)

Like a baby. Feel it.

RISTO

(*English*)

In English. Everything in English this morning. Got to practise.

One friend stands up and says, 'Shirt', handing Risto a brand-new shirt, still in its wrapper. Risto thanks him and takes a tie out of his own pocket. He takes off his jacket and T-shirt and starts to put on the shirt. He hangs the discarded clothes over the back of his chair. Another friend has a pair of cuff-links. Risto is particularly impressed with these. Finally, Jacket hands over his famous jacket. Risto is clearly close to overwhelmed.

JACKET

I bought it in Marks and Spencer. In Paris. They had lots in this style but only one in this colour. I love this colour.

RISTO

You're sure?

JACKET

Only because it's going to be on television. If I cannot be famous myself, my jacket can be.

Risto puts it on. He looks a million dollars. People wolf-whistle and so on.

RISTO

I must go.

He goes to check the time on the clock.

A watch. I need a watch.

Someone passes him a watch.

Thank you.

25

CUT TO:

EXT. HOLIDAY INN, SARAJEVO. MORNING.

Risto races across the rubble and goes in.

INT. LOBBY, HOLIDAY INN. MORNING.

Risto arriving at the hotel. He asks after Henderson at reception.

INT. BREAKFAST ROOM, HOLIDAY INN. MORNING.

A porter shows Risto into the breakfast room.

The place is heaving with journalists. Pick up on a French Journalist talking to a Canadian.

> FRENCH JOURNALIST
> I never wear protective clothing – or camouflage. I wear my hat. I drive an open-topped car. Dressed like that you might be a soldier. Dressed like this I am obviously a harmless journalist.

> CANADIAN
> The network want me to wear this flak jacket. I think it makes me look wussy. And fat too.

Jane is having breakfast with Flynn.

> FLYNN
> You look terrible.

> JANE
> Now I can tell you. I was a whiskey virgin until last night. Could you tell?

> FLYNN
> You looked like a woman of experience.

Risto approaches the table.

> RISTO
> Jane Carson?

26

JANE

Mr Risto? Please sit down. Michael will be with us in a
minute.

(*to Flynn*)

This is our new driver.

FLYNN

Nice to meet you. Like the jacket. Nice colour.

JANE

Yes, it's a great colour. Really. Unusual but not showy.

Zeljko, the waiter, approaches the table.

FLYNN

(*murmured to Zeljko*)

Did you get them?

ZELJKO

Four, sir.

Zeljko hands Flynn four eggs.

FLYNN

Genius.

Flynn hands Zeljko a packet of Marlboros.

ZELJKO

This is too much, sir. This will do nicely.

*He pockets four cigarettes and hands the rest of the packet back to
Flynn, who cracks one egg into a glass as he makes the next speech.*

FLYNN

For my head.

(*to Jane*)

You want one for your head?

*He swallows the egg and then cracks another into the glass. Risto is
looking at the eggs in a kind of rapture. Flynn feels the need to explain
himself.*

You don't happen to know anyone with a phone that works?

RISTO

All the phones in Sarajevo work.

FLYNN

Yeah. Inside Sarajevo. I was thinking about trying to contact that Outside World.

RISTO

In Sarajevo we no longer believe in the Outside World.

FLYNN

Could you use a hangover cure yourself?

RISTO

Would you mind if I saved it till later? I haven't started my hangover yet.

FLYNN

Sure. Take them both.

Pick up on Jane talking discreetly to Henderson as he comes into the breakfast room.

JANE

He's over at the table.

> HENDERSON

Can't it wait? I need some breakfast. Zjelko said there was a possibility of eggs.

He sees Zjelko, who comes over discreetly and takes two cigarettes from Henderson in exchange for two eggs.

> JANE

His English is good. He studied in Bristol or somewhere. For a year . . .

They are drifting over towards the table. Risto has got up and is heading for them with his hand outstretched. Henderson has to move his eggs to shake hands.

> RISTO

Mr Henderson.

> HENDERSON
> (*dismissive*)

How d'you do?
> (*to Jane*)

Looks like something out of Burton's window.

> RISTO

Marks and Spencer. Burton's do a jacket with a similar cut but only Marks and Spencer had it in this colour.

> HENDERSON
> (*smiles*)

You're hired. I'm sorry.

Greg comes running up. There is a sudden hubbub in the room.

What's going on?

> GREG

There's been some kind of attack. A mortar attack. It was on the radio.

> HENDERSON
> (*to Risto, too slowly*)

Do you know the way to Princip Street?

RISTO

Yes, of course.

Henderson moves off. Greg runs. Henderson pauses, looking at the pair of eggs in his hand.

HENDERSON

I was going to have these for breakfast but it looks like there won't be time . . . perhaps you'd . . .

RISTO

Thank you . . .

He automatically proffers a pair of cigarettes for them. Henderson, always anxious about the etiquette, takes them.

CUT TO:

INT. ASHA'S BAR. EVENING.

Risto arriving back at the café, looking tired and defeated. The jacket is folded carefully over his arm. Its owner – Jacket – is playing a big cello in the corner, accompanying another musician on the piano. When Jacket sees Risto he cheers. Risto starts to hand out some things he took from the hotel.

RISTO

Bosko. Some soap from the Hotel. Get a wash, then maybe she'll marry you.

JACKET

An egg. Thank you. Two eggs. Three eggs, three eggs is a miracle. Four. Four eggs. Is there a word for four eggs?

RISTO

Omelette.

JACKET

Of course it is. Asha! Where's Asha.

Pick up on Asha (pub owner) cooking an omelette behind the counter. The whole pub is gathered around the bar inhaling it.

BOSKO

You know, before the siege I didn't like eggs.

30

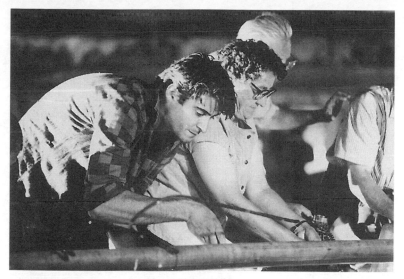

JACKET
Before the siege I didn't think about food at all.

The plate is put before Jacket on the table. He picks up the knife and fork with everyone looking at him. Then he puts them down again.

JACKET
I can't. Bosko . . . you first.

Bosko edges a corner off the omelette with a fork and eats it. He grins. Someone else takes another piece. The omelette gets passed around until it passes Risto.

RISTO
No. Thanks. The smell was enough. I'll wait till this is all over.

The omelette goes back to Jacket, who tucks in to what is left of it. Everyone crowds round. Risto pulls back a bit. Bosko talks to him.

BOSKO
Were you at the bread queue?

Risto nods. He looks haunted.

CUT TO:

3   Fucking Jane Austen

INT. RECEPTION, HOLIDAY INN. DAY.

Lots of journalists are piling out of the hotel. We are seeing the tail-end of the earlier Holiday Inn scene, with Risto following Henderson and Greg.

EXT. HOLIDAY INN, SARAJEVO. DAY

Henderson, Greg and Risto pile into the van. There are other cars pulling away from the front of the hotel. Henderson gets into the front next to Risto. As the van is about to pull off, a young woman knocks on the back window, opens the door and climbs in. Greg is taken aback.

> GREG
>
> Who are you?

> ANNIE
>
> Annie McGee. I haven't got a car. Well come on. Don't let me hold things up.

Greg and Risto look to Henderson for instructions.

> HENDERSON
>
> Just drive.

CUT TO:

INT. VAN. SARAJEVO. DAY.

Greg is trying to talk to Annie.

> GREG
>
> The Serbs have big guns in those hills up there. BM-40s I think. 122mm multiple launchers. Are you interested in artillery at all?

> ANNIE
>
> No.

35

She leans forward to talk to Henderson.

I'm working on this really big story. But to get it I need to get
out of Sarajevo. I need a car and I need someone with a bit of
clout.

*Henderson is not reacting. The van is stopping. They are in a town-
centre shopping street. There are cars parked at crazy angles
everywhere. People are running.*

EXT. STREETS, SARAJEVO. DAY.

Henderson gets out of the van. Annie follows, tagging along behind him.

ANNIE
This is the biggest story of the whole war. Just the worst, you
know.

HENDERSON
Worse than bombing people while they're queueing for
bread?

ANNIE
Way worse. Compared to this story, this thing is like . . .
fucking . . . Jane Austen.

HENDERSON
Really? I never fucked Jane Austen myself . . .

*As he says this, they are coming around the corner. They both stop dead
in their tracks.*

EXT. BREAD QUEUE SITE, SARAJEVO. DAY.

*They are in a small pedestrian precinct. There are shopping trolleys and
bags all over the place, frosted with broken glass like caster sugar. There
are also people, dozens of people, lying dead and horribly wounded, all
over the street. The sound of groaning and weeping fills the air. Now,
the date goes up.*

FEBRUARY 1994

Annie and Henderson are both staring, impotently entranced. All the other journalists are there, including Flynn and the Frenchman.

A small hatchback car backs into the precinct, almost knocking them both over. It parks sharply. The driver gets out and starts to help someone load one of the dead into the back of the car. Risto comes up behind Henderson. He stares in silence. Greg arrives and starts filming. A woman comes up and starts to shout at Greg's camera. He just films her.

> HENDERSON
> *(to Risto)*
> What is she saying?

Risto tries to collect himself.

> RISTO
> She is saying . . . she's upset and she's saying . . . she doesn't know what she's saying. She has lost her control. You shouldn't film her. Excuse me.

With a polite nod, Risto moves off and starts to try to help move the bodies into the civilian cars which are now manoeuvring into the precinct. Annie goes to help him. Henderson seems unsure what to do. Someone near him starts to lift a wounded man to his feet and Henderson helps get him up. The wounded man puts his arm round his friend's neck and they start to hobble off. Suddenly, the rattle of automatic-weapon fire splits the air. There is a scream and everyone hits the deck. There is a terrible moment of pause.

Henderson is lying flat on the ground. He looks up, tries to see what everyone else is doing. He finds he is next to a corpse.

Suddenly everyone seems to be on their feet, running for doorways, trying to get round the corner. The gunfire starts again.

Everyone is now flat against the walls and now there is a long, uncompromising burst of gunfire. Dust and glass whirl along the middle of the street. Henderson, Greg, Annie and Risto are all cowering in a doorway.

38

The gunfire stops. No one dares to breathe.

Henderson turns round to face the carnage – the bodies like bundles of rags. As he watches, an arm raises itself from one bundle and a weak voice calls out for help. Instinctively, he steps forward but then pulls back. He looks along the row of shop doorways. Everyone is looking at the arm, raised motionless in the air like the Lady of the Lake. The weak voice calls out for help again. It is a moment of agonising stasis. Two men run to move the body into one of the cars.

      CUT TO:

INT. HOSPITAL, SARAJEVO. DAY.

Hospital chaos. Trolleys whizzing everywhere. People crying. People trying to grab the attention of medics. Medics shrugging them off. A little boy wanders down the corridor, obviously looking for someone. The boy starts talking to Henderson. Risto comes over.

                  HENDERSON
What's he saying?

                  RISTO
He's lost. He's looking for his mother and father. He went with them this morning to buy bread. I'll ask him his name.
                  (does so)
Vladimir. He's a Serb.

Risto and Henderson look at each other, helplessly. Henderson shrugs. Greg starts to film. Risto is with Greg.

      CUT TO:

INT. HOSPITAL, SARAJEVO. DAY.

Greg's images of carnage.

INT. CORRIDOR, HOSPITAL. DAY.

Henderson and the boy, Vladimir, are sitting on a bench in an empty corridor. At the other end of the corridor, Risto appears in the company of a Doctor. The two are talking earnestly, quietly. When the doctor leaves, Risto comes to Henderson.

                    RISTO
    They're dead.

Involuntarily, they both look down at Vladimir. Vladimir looks up at Henderson, who shudders.

                  HENDERSON
    We'll have to tell him.

He looks at Risto, who is very uncomfortable.

    CUT TO:

INT. CORRIDOR, HOSPITAL. DAY.

Vladimir is sitting on a bench. Henderson is kneeling down in front of him, with his hands on the boy's shoulders. He is telling him that his parents are dead. Risto translates for him. Vladimir looks completely blank at the news.

                  HENDERSON
                  (to Risto)
    Are you sure he understands this?

Risto asks Vladimir if he understands.

                  VLADIMIR
                  (Bosnian)
    What do I do now?

Henderson looks to Risto for a translation.

                    RISTO
                  (to Henderson) ·
    He says, what does he do now?

                    GREG
    Has he got any relatives? We could take him to his family.

Risto explains this to Vladimir in Bosnian. Vladimir carries on talking.

                    RISTO
    He just keeps saying, help me. Can you help me?

                  HENDERSON
    Ask him if he has any family. We can give him a lift.

Risto translates. Vladimir looks Henderson in the eye, then gets up from the bench and walks away down the long hospital corridor. Henderson's hands flop down uselessly. He stands up to watch the boy go. Vladimir does not look back at him.

The best way we can help is by getting the news out.

> GREG
> Nothing. I mean, sure. You're right.

CUT TO:

INT. EDIT SUITE. TV CENTRE. EVENING.

Jane is birding the report back to England. Greg is helping. Henderson is furious. Jane is tired, tense, preoccupied.

> HENDERSON
> Are you seriously telling me that this is not the lead story tonight?

> JANE
> No, this is not the lead story.

> HENDERSON
> And would you care to tell me what *is* the lead story? The Second Coming?

> JANE
> The Duke and Duchess of York are getting divorced. Or separated. Not sure which.

Henderson walks out of the room. Jane growls.

CUT TO:

INT. CORRIDOR, TV CENTRE. EVENING.

Henderson walking away from his edit suite. Jane appears from the room behind him. Henderson passes Flynn, who is carrying a paper cup.

> FLYNN
> Hey, Michael. I hear your network had a big scoop today. A royals story. The Duke and Duchess of Pork.

41

Henderson breezes past. Flynn talks to Jane.

You know all the time I was in that hospital, I had a feeling I was in the wrong place.

                          JANE
What did your lot lead on?

                          FLYNN
The Superbowl.

CUT TO:

EXT. TV CENTRE. SARAJEVO. EVENING.

Henderson walking to the van. Risto is waiting.

                          HENDERSON
I'll drive.

He gets in on the driver's side. Risto gets in next to him. The van edges out into the road.

                          RISTO
Wait. Look.

Someone is lashing a crude sign to a lamppost. It's like a road sign but it shows a sniper. There are similar signs lashed to every lamppost along the road.

Snipers.

Henderson thinks.

                          HENDERSON
Fine.

He slams his foot down on the accelerator and the van screams off along Snipers' Alley.

CUT TO:

EXT. BURNING HOUSE. DAY.

A house on fire. Children running away from the explosion.

CUT TO:

INT. HENDERSON'S BEDROOM, HOLIDAY INN. NIGHT.

We are in Henderson's nightmare. He sits up suddenly, sweaty and breathless. He is fully clothed, lying on top of the bed. A half-empty whiskey bottle is on the bedside table. He looks around the room. Distant sound of artillery. And over that sound, the ringing of childish laughter again. Henderson cradles his head in his hands, trying to cut out the sound.

He stands up, drags the mattress off the bed and carts it over to the window. He hoists the mattress up to the window, planning to stuff the window with the mattress. The sound of laughter is growing all the time.

At the last moment, Henderson looks out of the window.

    CUT TO:

EXT. STREET, SARAJEVO. NIGHT.

Henderson's POV: *There far below him he sees not the Altar Boy he feared but two teenage girls, talking to some soldiers. They are laughing and flirting. Cigarettes are handed over.*

    CUT TO:

INT. HENDERSON'S BEDROOM, HOLIDAY INN. NIGHT.

Henderson leans his forehead against the window, relieved. He watches the girls.

    CUT TO:

EXT. STREET, SARAJEVO. NIGHT.

Henderson's POV: Pick up on the girls. One of them is called Lucky Strike.

    CUT TO:

EXT. STREET, SARAJEVO. NIGHT.

Lucky Strike is giggling. She gives the soldier a peck on the cheek, then she laughs some more. Lucky Strike and the other girl run away laughing into the night. Cannon fire illuminates the ruins.

CUT TO:

4 The Price of Cigarettes

INT. DORMITORY, LJUBICA IVEZIC ORPHANAGE. NIGHT.

A ten-year-old girl is lying on her bed in a huge, dank dormitory at the orphanage. Her name is Emira. Not too distant pounding of artillery. The flickering of explosions plays across the ceiling.

Somewhere downstairs a baby starts crying. Emira hears it, slides out of bed.

    CUT TO:

INT. STAIRWAY, ORPHANAGE. NIGHT.

Emira goes down some stairs, collecting a little torch from a shelf on the way. Her movements are routine. She has done this a million times. She goes down to the cellar.

    CUT TO:

47

INT. CELLAR, ORPHANAGE. NIGHT.

The torchlight is feeble and circumscribed but bright enough for us to see that she is walking past a phalanx of cots. Each cot has two babies, sleeping top-to-tail. There are six or seven cots in this windowless cellar. Eventually she finds the one that is crying and picks it up. The baby is wearing a sleep suit with the Roadrunner cartoon character on it.

Emira opens a cupboard. It is full of powdered baby milk. She starts to prepare it, taking water from a big barrel.

Suddenly, there is a rap on the window and an urgent whisper from outside. Emira opens the window. Lucky Strike crawls in.

The following conversation takes place in Bosnian and is subtitled.

> LUCKY STRIKE
> *(Bosnian)*

Look.

She reaches inside her blouse and produces three filter-tip cigarettes.

> EMIRA
> *(Bosnian)*

They're not real. They're Drinas.

> LUCKY STRIKE
> *(Bosnian)*

Oh yeah? Smell.

She lights up the cigarette on the twig-burning stove.

Smell America.
> *(long drags)*

Micky Mouse. Dollar bill.

> EMIRA
> *(Bosnian)*

You're not going to smoke it?

> LUCKY STRIKE
> *(Bosnian)*

Plenty more where this came from.

48

(*more drags*)
Hollywood. New York City. Big Mac. You come with me
next time.

EMIRA
(*Bosnian*)

I don't think so.

LUCKY STRIKE
(*Bosnian*)

Why not? He asked me if I had friends.
(*more drags*)
River Phoenix. Keanu Reeves. The Partridge Family with
David Cassidy. He's in love with me.

EMIRA
(*Bosnian*)

Who?

LUCKY STRIKE
(*Bosnian*)

Someone. He's a film producer. He's going to put me in a
movie.

EMIRA
(*Bosnian*)

Obviously.

LUCKY STRIKE
(*Bosnian*)

You'll see.

There is a sound from outside. Lucky Strike panics and curses.

Savic.

*She tries to pinch out the cigarette but burns her finger and ends up
dropping it on the floor. She runs for the other door.*

Say a word and I'll kill you. I swear. I'll kill you.

*She dives out through the other door. Emira goes and stands carefully
on the tip of the cigarette. The door bursts open and a serious torch
floods the room with chemical brilliance. Instinctively Emira shields the*

baby's eyes rather than her own. The torch carrier is Mrs Savic, a strong, middle-aged woman, full of emotional intelligence but now exhausted.

MRS SAVIC
(snarling in Bosnian)
Who's that?

EMIRA
(Bosnian)
It's me. I didn't want to wake the others.

MRS SAVIC
(Bosnian)
Emira, I'm sorry. I thought there was someone here.

EMIRA
(Bosnian)
He never sleeps properly. Usually I end up taking him into my bed. Come on, Roadrunner.

MRS SAVIC
(Bosnian)
Good night.

She goes to kiss Emira, then stops.

You've been smoking.

EMIRA
(Bosnian)
Just a Drina.

Mrs Savic has pushed Emira away from her during this exchange. Emira loses her footing a little and the cigarette is revealed.

MRS SAVIC
(Bosnian)
This is a real cigarette.

EMIRA
(Bosnian)
No, it's just a Drina.

MRS SAVIC
(*Bosnian*)
I smoke Drinas. They don't smell like this.
(*shouts*)
Where did you get it?

EMIRA
(*Bosnian*)
Don't shout. You'll scare him.

MRS SAVIC
(*Bosnian*)
I know how much a cigarette like this costs. I know you've got
no money. There is only one way you could have got this. I
know the price a girl like you would have to pay for a cigarette
like this. Tell me where you've been. With soldiers? Tell me.
Tell me or so help me –

EMIRA
(*Bosnian*)
I'm going to bed.

*She tries to leave but Mrs Savic stands in front of her and then slaps her
across the face. The baby starts to cry. Emira just stares at her. Mrs
Savic quakes.*

(*icy*)
Good-night.

*She walks past Mrs Savic. Mrs Savic sighs, curses herself for her quick
temper. She slumps in the chair, considers the cigarette and, after a
moment or two, lights it up.*

CUT TO:

EXT. ORPHANAGE. MORNING.

*Henderson's car has pulled up. It is a cold morning. Greg, Risto and
Henderson get out. Greg starts to unload camera equipment.*

CUT TO:

INT. DORMITORY, ORPHANAGE. MORNING.

Emira is looking out of the window of her dormitory. Down below she sees Greg pulling out the camera and Mrs Savic greeting Henderson. Emira is amazed. She looks around at Lucky Strike, who is sitting on the end of her bed, fixing her hair, bursting with vanity. She glances out of the window. She speaks with airy self-confidence.

LUCKY STRIKE
(*Bosnian*)

Ah. They're here. Goodbye.

She heads off, but can't resist looking back.

That'll teach you not to believe me.

End on Emira's astonishment.

CUT TO:

EXT. ORPHANAGE. MORNING.

Some of the children from the orphanage are grouped outside, standing behind Mrs Savic; others are cutting down a big tree. Henderson is setting up a shot. Greg is smoking a cigarette while he waits. The children stand in neat rows, the big ones carrying babies, but all eyes are fixed on Greg's cigarettes. Emira tries to get all the children neatly lined up, like a wedding photographer.

Finally Emira is ready for a take.

HENDERSON

OK, Greg.

Greg gets his camera ready and drops his cigarette. Immediately, all the neatly arranged children dive out of their lines and pounce on the cigarette. Mrs Savic starts yelling.

GREG

Shit. Sorry. Forgot.

Henderson is amused. He notices that one girl has not moved. She stands staring fixedly at him. It's Emira. He smiles at her while Mrs Savic whips everyone else into line and confiscates the cigarette. Emira does not react.

52

INT. EDIT SUITE, TV CENTRE. DAY.

ON MONITOR: EXT. ORPHANAGE (REPORT). DAY.

Jane, Henderson and Greg are editing the report on the orphanage. On the monitor is the shot we saw being set up, the shot of all the children outside the orphanage. Jane is holding a flak jacket.

> JANE
> I really think you should wear one. Both of you.

> GREG
> I don't mind. I quite like them.

Henderson remains absorbed in the report.

> HENDERSON
> Before the siege, she was only taking in babies. So some of these children grew up there.

> JANE
> Everyone else is wearing them. I don't even know if we can get insured without one. Even Flynn is wearing one.

> HENDERSON
> Even Flynn. My God.

> JANE
> Look, Michael, I know you're going to make a fuss about this. I know you don't like them.

> HENDERSON
> Sssh. Listen . . .

He points to the screen where Mrs Savic is walking into the garden of the orphanage. She points to three little gravestones.

> MRS SAVIC
> (*On monitor*)
> When they bombed us, three children died. These are their graves . . .

Henderson looks round at Jane, who has gone quiet.

HENDERSON
I like flak jackets. I think they're wonderful. I think everyone
should have one. Everyone in Sarajevo should have a flak
jacket. That's what I think.

Go in on the monitor where Mrs Savic is at the graveside again.

MRS SAVIC
(*Bosnian*)
I bury these children here in the garden. Here everyone can
see. We are dying. I will not put them away out of sight.
Everyone must know. Tell them. Tell them. Keep on telling
them until – I hope – they will move us . . .

CUT TO:

MONTAGE.

Politicians talking about the situation in Sarajevo.

EXT. AIRPORT, SARAJEVO. DAY.

*An RAF Hercules coming in to land. It is a massive plane. The date
goes up on screen.*

JUNE 16TH 1992

CUT TO:

EXT. AIRPORT. SARAJEVO. DAY.

*Henderson, Risto and Greg are waiting with lots of other journalists to
have their papers checked at the entrance to the airport.*

RISTO
Jammy Dodgers. That is what impressed me about England.
You know Jammy Dodgers? Round biscuits with jam inside.
And Mars Bars.

GREG
There's a Mars Bar now and instead of fondant inside, it's got
ice cream.

RISTO

No. You're lying.

GREG

Absolutely. They taste best if you let them go a little bit soft.

RISTO

And they say there is no God!

Their papers are cleared. They are waved forward.

CUT TO:

5 The Cleanest People I Ever Saw

EXT. AIRPORT, SARAJEVO. DAY.

The RAF Hercules is touching down. The journalists huddle together.

Greg is putting on the flak jacket.

> GREG
> (*to Risto*)

What do you think?

> RISTO

Good.

> HENDERSON

You can have mine if you like.

> RISTO

This is my best suit. I'm not going to hide it under an armour-plated anorak.

Pick up on the VIPs, who are getting off the plane. They are beautifully groomed and neat, like a posse of bridegrooms.

Flynn has popped up behind Annie.

> FLYNN

Jeez those guys are clean. I don't think I ever saw such clean-looking people.

> ANNIE

They wash their hands a lot, I know that. I thought you went to see Michael Jackson.

> FLYNN

Couldn't get a ticket. Anyway, got a better offer. This millionaire guy has put up a shit-load of money for Bobby Fischer to play Boris Spassky again. It's down at the seaside somewhere. Want to come?

A UN jeep scrambles up to meet the VIPs. Journalists shout questions about air strikes, peace talks and so on. Pick up on Henderson in the throng. He is shouting a question and being jostled.

HENDERSON
Have you got any plans to evacuate the sick, or the children? Do you realize that hospitals and orphanages are being shelled daily . . .?

The VIP glides past Henderson, passing close enough to be thumped.

VIP
We're here to consider a range of options . . .

And then he's gone. Most of the journalists follow, leaving Henderson alone on the tarmac, close to the big plane.

HENDERSON
Is that thing flying out of here empty?

Greg looks over at the plane.

CUT TO:

INT. RAF HERCULES, AIRPORT. DAY.

Henderson inside the cavernous fuselage of the Hercules. He talks straight to camera.

HENDERSON
It's extraordinary, is it not, that this plane will fly out of here empty when there are children trapped in the most dangerous corner of the most dangerous city on earth. It would be a simple matter to move them. But somebody, somewhere along the bureaucratic line is saying no.

CUT TO:

STOCK FOOTAGE.

The footage of Bhoutros Bhoutros Ghali telling the people of Sarajevo that they have got things out of proportion. There are fourteen places in the world worse than Sarajevo.

CUT TO:

INT. PRESS CONFERENCE. DAY.

Shot of Flynn standing up in a crowded room to ask a question of the (unseen) UN Secretary General.

>   FLYNN
> Could you tell us what the other fourteen places are? Just so
> we know. And do you think Sarajevo is moving up or down
> the table?

CUT TO:

INT. EDITING SUITE, TV CENTRE. DAY.

EXT. ORPHANAGE (REPORT). DAY.

The continuation of Henderson's report. A young boy is talking straight to camera. What he says in Croatian is shadowed by a voice-over translation by Risto.

>   BRANKO
>   (*Bosnian*)
> My name is Branko. I am seven. I want to see my mother
> again soon.

He smiles for the camera and, during the pause, Henderson's voice adds a gloss:

>   HENDERSON
>   (*voice-over*)
> Branko's mother was killed by a shell.

Next, a Muslim girl, Muneera.

>   MUNEERA
>   (*Bosnian*)
> I want to live on a farm, with a donkey and cows and some
> plum trees.

>   HENDERSON
>   (*voice-over*)
> Muneera's family are Muslim farmers. Their farm was taken
> away during the ethnic cleansing. No one knows where her
> parents are.

The next child up is Emira.

EMIRA
(Bosnian)

My name is Emira. I have been here a long time but now I would like to leave. I was born on a farm. We had a donkey. One day some soldiers came . . .

CUT TO:

INT. ORPHANAGE. DAY.

Emira is being filmed by Greg. She is telling her story with manic animation and sound effects. The story is subtitled. Risto is at first whispering his translation to Henderson but after a while he stops.

EMIRA
(Bosnian)

The soldiers came and took away my father. My mother was very upset, then a big bomb came through the roof, so we had to run away with my brothers. Then they all stepped on land-mines and they were blown sky-high except my mother and she was run over by a tank! Then there were some wolves . . .

Risto looks bemused.

RISTO

Are you sure?

Henderson and Risto are laughing.

CUT TO:

INT. MRS SAVIC'S OFFICE, ORPHANAGE. DAY.

One wall of the office is covered in photographs of children. Mrs Savic is talking to Risto and Henderson. She has her hand on Emira's shoulder.

MRS SAVIC

She was brought here when she was only a few months old. She has been with me all her life. Illegitimate children are considered a great disgrace here. No one has ever wanted Emira.

62

Emira hands something to Henderson. It is a drinks coaster with a smudgy reproduction of the Haywain on it. She asks Henderson something in Bosnian.

RISTO

She wants to know if this is where you come from?

HENDERSON

Yes. More or less. It's changed slightly since then of course.

EMIRA
(Bosnian)

Good. That's where I want to go.
(to Risto)
Tell him he can keep the picture for a present. If he comes back tomorrow.

Henderson wants to know what she said.

RISTO

She wants you to come back tomorrow.

Emira keeps talking. This is also subtitled.

EMIRA
(Bosnian)

I want to go away from here. I want to go to England.

RISTO
(English)

She says she wants to get out of Sarajevo.

MRS SAVIC
(Bosnian)

He's going to get us all out of here. When people see his film, they'll help. I know they will.
(to Henderson in English)
I said your film would get us out of here. Is it right?

HENDERSON

I hope so.

EMIRA
(*Bosnian*)
Did he say yes? Did he promise?

RISTO
She wants a promise.

HENDERSON
It's a promise. I'm going to make it impossible for them to leave without doing something.

RISTO
(*Bosnian*)
He promises.

Henderson is invigorated, full of purpose.

CUT TO:

INT. BAR, HOLIDAY INN. EVENING.

Henderson, Annie and Jane are sharing a drink and talking discreetly.

JANE
Annie has this amazing story . . .

ANNIE
I've been working on it for weeks. Now I' m ready to roll with it. I know my source is good . . .

HENDERSON
And . . .

JANE
I've got a letter of passage from Sonia Karadic. It means we can go behind the Serb lines. We can use this. Take Annie with you and go with her story.

HENDERSON
What're you talking about? We've got a story. A big story. We've got fifty kids staring down the barrel of a gun. How big a story do you want?

JANE
We've done that story.

64

HENDERSON

Oh no, no, no. We've *started* that story. We haven't done it. As
long as the UN are here, we're keeping the kids on screen. Every
night a different kid, same message. Get me out of here. I am
going to make it impossible for them to leave those kids behind.

JANE

That's not news, that's a campaign.

HENDERSON

I don't care what it is. I'm going to get those kids out. Come
on. What are you worried about? It's got cute little kids, big
guns, evil bureaucrats. It's great television.

JANE

If it works.

HENDERSON

It'll work. Trust me. It'll work.

He gets up to leave.

EXT. UN BUILDING, SARAJEVO. DAY.

*Risto and Henderson are talking near the van. Greg comes running out
excitedly.*

GREG

Mike! This is it. They're going to visit the orphanage.

HENDERSON

Who?

GREG

The working party. It's happening. You cracked it.

*Henderson doesn't reply. He jumps into the van and Risto follows, starts
the van up and off they go.*

INT. ORPHANAGE. DAY.

*Mrs Savic is a whirlwind of organization, directing the children around
the orphanage, getting it ready. Floors and faces washed. Kitchen and
hair tidied. Henderson talks quietly to Mrs Savic.*

65

HENDERSON
Maybe . . . it would be better if they didn't look *too* neat.
We're trying to get their sympathy . . .

MRS SAVIC
These are orphans, Mr Henderson. Not beggars.

She hurries on.

CUT TO:

EXT. ORPHANAGE. DAY.

A UN flag is hung out of the window.

CUT TO:

INT. TV ROOM, ORPHANAGE. DAY.

*The children end up spruce and expectant, watching TV. Mrs Savic
comes in and realizes they are watching a slasher movie. She switches it
off and replaces it with a wildlife documentary. Henderson laughs.*

CUT TO:

INT./EXT. RAF HERCULES, AIRPORT. DAY.

*The UN working party we saw arriving earlier is filing onto the plane.
Their suits are clean and their shirts are not sweaty. Not a hair is out of
place.*

*They move into the body of the plane and assume their seats. There are
only five of them. In the vast spaces of the plane, they look lost and silly.*

EXT. RAF HERCULES, AIRPORT. DAY.

*The Hercules takes off. The plane moves easily away into the sky,
leaving Sarajevo very far behind.*

CUT TO:

INT. ORPHANAGE. DAY.

*The children now restless in front of the TV. They start shouting and
brawling. One of them gets up and changes back to the slasher movie.*

*Henderson and Mrs Savic leave the room, resigned. Emira watches
Henderson, troubled.*

CUT TO:

INT. BREAKFAST ROOM, HOLIDAY INN. MORNING.

*An exhausted and demoralized Henderson is shoving his breakfast
round on the plate. Jane is trying to cheer him up.*

JANE
They were still great reports. The audience feedback we got
was . . . unbelievable and according to –

HENDERSON
This coffee's freezing. Where's Zeljko?

JANE
I know you must be disappointed but –

HENDERSON
So what do we do now? Go with Annie and the story to end
all stories?

JANE
(*not looking him in the eye*)
Annie's . . . not around.

EXT. BOSNIAN COUNTRYSIDE. DAY.

*Flynn is driving his car. Annie is sitting next to him. A cameraman is
in the back of the car. Annie is gazing out at the beautiful countryside.
Soon they will come to a village.*

ANNIE
You must have heard of it. The Archers. It's a soap opera in
Britain.

FLYNN
I never watch TV. I hate TV except when I'm on it.

ANNIE
This is radio. When the Archers started there was no such
thing as TV. It's about farming.

FLYNN
What, so you listen to people dipping sheep?

ANNIE
Exactly. The sheep are the best thing. It's the same sheep every week. It's got two different bleats, one for comedy and one for tragedy.

FLYNN
I hate animals. I hate animals and I hate people who keep animals. My father had a dog.

ANNIE
And he loved it more than he loved you.

FLYNN
No. He hated the dog. A huge dog. He bought it so he'd get some exercise. It dragged him round everywhere. He couldn't keep up with it. In the end, he had a heart attack. I blame the dog.

CUT TO:

6   Sitting Ducks

EXT. STREETS, SARAJEVO. EVENING.

Dusk is gathering. Greg is driving frantically.

> GREG
> Shit. It's getting dark. I've had all I can take of Sarajevo nightlife.

> HENDERSON
> Go past the orphanage.

> GREG
> Can't we just get home. Once it gets dark round here . . .

> HENDERSON
> The orphanage is on the way home.

CUT TO:

EXT. STREETS, SARAJEVO. NIGHT.

It is dark. A shell explodes in the air. For a split second, the whole city bursts into visibility. Then it goes dark again. The ITN car flares into visibility in the explosion of light. It swerves into a side road.

EXT. CHECKPOINTS/STREETS, SARAJEVO. NIGHT.

The car emerges in another road, near a checkpoint.

> HENDERSON
> Here. Here. Go this way. Past the orphanage.

CUT TO:

EXT. LJUBICA IVEZIC ORPHANAGE. NIGHT.

A shot of the shell-damaged orphanage. As we watch, a wall collapses and a small fire starts. The ITN car pulls up.

CUT TO:

INT. CELLAR, ORPHANAGE. NIGHT.

The babies are being passed up a human chain with Henderson at one end and Mrs Savic at the other. When the Roadrunner baby gets to Emira, she keeps hold of him, cuddling him. The others are passed on. The noise of shelling is nightmarish in its insistence and its proximity. The howling of babies is infernal.

CUT TO:

INT. STAIRWAY, ORPHANAGE. NIGHT.

Pick up Henderson bringing a baby up the stairs. He looks up to see who is there to take it. There, above him, staring down at him from the top of the stairs, is Emira.

                        HENDERSON
Emira . . .?

She turns away from him.

                        HENDERSON
Emira . . .

She looks him in the eye and turns her head.

CUT TO:

INT. HENDERSON'S BEDROOM, HOLIDAY INN. NIGHT.

Henderson sprawled full-length on his bed. There is a big bag of dirty washing on the floor next to the bed. There is a knock on the door. It is Zeljko.

                        ZELJKO
I thought you might like to know; the washing machines are working, sir.¨

                        HENDERSON
Zeljko, angels sent you.

Henderson collects his washing with some distaste and then goes.

CUT TO:

INT. LAUNDRY ROOM, HOLIDAY INN. NIGHT.

The room is crowded with journalists, all crowding for position on the driers. Greg greets him.

> GREG
> Don't get excited. There's only one working.

Pick up on two American journalists talking.

> AMERICAN ONE
> Why would anyone steal your wet socks?

> AMERICAN TWO
> They're my lucky socks. If I don't find them, I'm going to get shot.

> GREG
> Excuse me, I couldn't help overhearing you mention lucky socks. I have lucky socks too.

Suddenly, there is an excited shuffling as two new people come into the room. They are Flynn and Annie. People crowd around them. Henderson finds Jane and corners her.

> HENDERSON
> Can I talk to you? It's about one of the kids in the orphanage.

> JANE
> Oh, for crying out loud, Michael, haven't you heard? You haven't heard, have you?

She pushes past Henderson and gives Annie a hug. Henderson is left face to face with Flynn.

> HENDERSON
> I thought you were covering some chess game.

> FLYNN
> Met a lady who needed a lift.

> HENDERSON
> (realizing)
> Annie got her story.

He nods his head.

CUT TO:

CONCENTRATION CAMP FOOTAGE. DAY.

This should be newsreel footage. It should just blow into the middle of the film like a bitter wind.

CUT TO:

INT. CORRIDOR, TV CENTRE, SARAJEVO. NIGHT.

A chaotic scrabble for phones and footage. Jane is yelling frantically into a phone. Pick up Henderson walking in with Greg.

HENDERSON
Where did this lot come from?

GREG
I hope they've bought their own bog roll with them, that's all I know.

Flynn goes past them.

HENDERSON
Errm . . . Flynn.

Flynn looks round.

I liked . . . I mean . . . it was a good report. Congratulations.

FLYNN
Thanks. Have you got any petrol?

Flynn moves on. Henderson looks confused.

CUT TO:

EXT. STREETS, SARAJEVO. DAWN.

Henderson and Flynn are in the ITN car. Flynn is looking at a scribbled map. Henderson turns left.

CUT TO:

EXT. BAKERY/STREETS, SARAJEVO. DAWN.

They pass a small bakery.

FLYNN

This is it. It's a bakery.

They pull up, get out of the car and go towards the bakery. Flynn stands still.

Listen. All quiet. Always goes quiet about five o'clock in the morning.

HENDERSON

Even they can't keep firing and drinking all night.

FLYNN

I like to think of them lying up there under the stars, sweetly plastered on Slivovitz, not a care in the world.

He knocks on the bakery door. A woman Baker answers. Flynn says a few words in Bosnian and hands over a polaroid photograph. The Baker puts her hand to her face, looks at the photograph for a while then asks them in.

CUT TO:

INT. BAKERY, SARAJEVO. DAWN.

Henderson and Flynn are sitting at a long, plain wooden table. The ovens are blazing in the background. A man is kneading dough with one hand. His other hand rests on the shoulder of his wife, the Baker woman. Flynn has a little package containing mouldy photographs and an identity card.

FLYNN

It's their son. He was in the camp. Behind the wire. I spoke to him. He gave me this address. Asked me to let them know he was alright.

The Baker woman gives them each a cake.

FLYNN

Promised me a cake in return.

HENDERSON
How can they be baking cakes when there's no bread?

FLYNN
It's for a christening.

HENDERSON
Flynn, am I hearing things or do you speak Bosnian?

FLYNN
I'm picking it up. I know when I try to describe this stuff in
English it doesn't sound real. I thought if any language in the
world had words for all this, Bosnian would be the one.

HENDERSON
Does it?

FLYNN
I don't know. I'm still on, Dubrovnik is popular for holidays.
The boulevard is very wide. The baker's wife is also very
wide.

HENDERSON
I can't eat this.

FLYNN
I think we have to eat it. I think it's important.

They start to eat the cakes.

CUT TO:

EXT. STREETS, SARAJEVO. DAY.

Jane and Risto walking along the boulevard.

CUT TO:

INT. RISTO'S FLAT. DAY.

*The screen is filled with a blazing illuminated twelfth-century image of
Moses parting the waters.*

*Open out and we are in Risto's neat, tiny flat with Risto, Jane, Jacket,
Bosko and Admira.*

A coffee-table book is open on his table. Risto is talking Jane through it.
It is a glossy reproduction of a medieval Jewish manuscript.

RISTO

It's twelfth century. Sephardic. When the Jews were expelled
from Spain, they brought it here with them. It's a Haggadah.
You use it at Passover. It's the story of the Exodus. It was in
the National Museum. When the Nazis came, it disappeared.
As soon as the War was over, it was back in the museum.
Now it's disappeared again.

JANE

It's lovely.

RISTO

On the real one, you can see wine stains and fingerprints,
where it has been used. People say that after this war it will
come back. In fact it has been sold to buy weapons.

*He rips a beautifully coloured page out from the back and uses it to light
the fire.*

JANE

What are you doing?!

RISTO

I use books to cook with. It's all there is. If you have to burn
your books, you should at least enjoy it. Special occasion.
Special book. Besides I could never relate to the Exodus. The
beginning yes. The city plagued with death and locusts but all
that stuff about leaving. If you want to burn a book yourself,
please be my guest.

She goes to the bookshelves.

I have my clothes, some of my books. My records. Speak
languages. But I live in the Stone Age. No electricity. No
running water. I'm a Stone Age sophisticate.

JANE

I never burnt a book in my life.

RISTO

There's a little bit of the Nazi in all of us.

Pick up on one of the images from the Haggadah again. An image of the Pharaoh's army in pursuit and then in defeat.

Risto is showing Jacket, and Bosko and Admira – a young couple – into the room. Admira shakes hands with Jane. Jacket is carrying his cello.

RISTO

They're going to get married.

JANE

Congratulations.

JACKET

I want to be on TV. Big star. Can you do that for me?

JANE

I can try. What do you do?

JACKET

I'm a great musician. Is it true?

RISTO

He's tone deaf.

78

JACKET

You know what I'm going to do? I'm going to give a concert here in Sarajevo.

JANE

Really? Is that a good idea?

JACKET

I will defy death in the name of art.

JANE

What about the audience?

JACKET

They will die happy listening to me. I'm not going to do it yet. You know Sarajevo is only the fifteenth worst place on earth? I am going to wait until we are number one.

Pick up on them all sitting down around the table.

ADMIRA

We wanted to get married since school but then the war came.

BOSKO

My family are Serbs. They left Sarajevo. Trouble with the neighbours. I stayed to be with Admira.

ADMIRA

I'm Muslim. When we met, it was normal for a Muslim girl to marry a Serb man. In Sarajevo anyway. Many marriages were mixed. But now it's impossible . . .

CUT TO:

7 An Old-fashioned Love Story

INT. BREAKFAST ROOM, HOLIDAY INN. DAY.

The breakfast room is at least ten times fuller than usual. Journalists of every nationality are complaining about the lack of food.

                    JANE
    It's a story about what it's like to live in a siege.

                    HENDERSON
            (*looking around the newly crowded dining room*)
    Look at them, they're like vultures.

                    JANE
    Are you listening to me?

                    HENDERSON
    Yes, yes. It was something about Love Across the Barricades.

                    JANE
    If you don't want to do it.

                    HENDERSON
    Whatever we do it makes no difference. It might as well be a love story.

INT. ABANDONED FLAT, SARAJEVO. DAY

(HENDERSON'S REPORT ON BOSKO AND ADMIRA)

Admira is emptying her handbag. There is a photograph of her parents. A cinema ticket – souvenir of her first date. A lock of hair. Other bits and pieces of somebody's life.

                    HENDERSON
                    (*voice-over*)
    . . . a lock of hair. A cinema ticket. A photograph of her parents. This is all that Admira will be able to take with her when she goes. She and Bosko have bribed the local Serb commander with cigarettes.

Admira starts to talk to camera. Her voice is shadowed by Risto's translation.

ADMIRA (*Bosnian*)/RISTO (*English*)
My mother used to say her life was in her handbag. I wanted to see how much of my life would fit in mine. It's all I will be able to take.

When she has finished speaking, she looks into the camera for a while. Stay on her face.

ADMIRA
(*Bosnian*)
Is that enough?

CUT TO:

INT. ABANDONED FLAT, SARAJEVO. DAY.

A bare, unfurnished, shell-damaged flat. Bosko and Admira look nervous. Greg is taking down his camera.

GREG
(*to Admira*)
We'll send you the tape for your wedding video.

BOSKO
Thank you.

Admira smiles. She is very nervous.

BOSKO
(*to Henderson*)
I have saw. Seen? Seen. News of Ten. Ha ha. Bong! Bong! Very good.

Bosko comes and shakes hands enthusiastically with Henderson, who looks slightly discomforted.

HENDERSON
Thank you.

CUT TO:

EXT./INT. ABANDONED FLAT. DAY.

Bosko and Admira carrying a couple of plastic bags towards a bridge. We are watching them from the window of the dilapidated flat. They look very small and vulnerable.

We watch the couple make their way towards the bridge. The space around them in nerve-rackingly empty.

> RISTO
> A strange kind of wedding march.

They get to the edge of the bridge and wait. They look around.

> RISTO
> Someone from the Serb side will come to meet them now. Look, the car.

On the other side of the bridge, the doors of an old Trabant open. A man in fatigues steps out of the back. Admira and Bosko go forward. Bosko looks back briefly. Then he falls, shot in the neck.

CUT QUICK TO:

EXT. BRIDGE, SARAJEVO. DAY.

A very tight shot of Admira screaming a blood-curdling scream. She turns to go, then falls, having been shot in the leg.

She turns back to the body of Bosko. She drags herself to the body, takes its head in her hands and caresses its hair, kisses its forehead. She is then shot in the chest.

CUT TO:

INT./EXT. STAIRWAY, ABANDONED FLATS. DAY.

Hand-held chaos. Stairs flick past. Henderson's back. Risto's voice. We are in the middle of the confusion and panic unleashed by the shooting. The crew are trying to leave the building.

CUT TO:

INT./EXT. ABANDONED FLATS. DAY.

Henderson runs away from us towards the bridge.

> RISTO
> (*shouting*)

STOP!

Henderson stops. Looks round. Looks back at Risto.

CUT TO:

EXT. BRIDGE, SARAJEVO. DAY.

A long lens shot of the bodies on the bridge. Henderson in the foreground, in front of the picture. He looks tense, haggard. Voices are lowered. We are looking at Greg's News Shot.

> GREG
> (*almost a whisper, behind camera*)

OK. That looks OK. Go for it . . .

> HENDERSON

Admira . . . and Bosko . . . behind me on the bridge are . . . Admira and Bosko and . . . I can't do it. I can't think of anything to say.

CUT TO:

EXT. BRIDGE, SARAJEVO. DAY.

(HENDERSON'S FINISHED REPORT ON ADMIRA AND BOSKO.)

Henderson is in front of the camera. The bridge and the bodies are way off behind him.

> HENDERSON

. . . That was twenty-four hours ago. No one will dare move the bodies. They stay on the bridge, a warning to anyone who thinks that the tolerant, cosmopolitan Sarajevo of old is still alive. A notice to those who think that love or hope can get you out of here.

CUT TO:

86

8 A Journey Home

INT. HENDERSON'S BEDROOM, HOLIDAY INN. NIGHT.

Flynn marks his bottle of whiskey. Henderson is packing.

FLYNN

When's your flight?

HENDERSON

Tomorrow night. Want these?

He throws him a large carton of duty-free cigarettes.

FLYNN

We should smoke them all.

HENDERSON

I don't smoke.

FLYNN

Me neither. Maybe it's time we started.

INT. HENDERSON'S BEDROOM, HOLIDAY INN. NIGHT.

Later that night, Henderson and Flynn are sitting in front of the TV.
They are both smoking heavily but without expertise. Sometimes two
cigarettes at a time. Sometimes they leave half the fag.

FLYNN

Let's go home. In fact, I am going home. I am going home
and I'm going to cover the New Hampshire primaries. No.
Too cold. The Superbowl. That's it.

HENDERSON

Tell me something. Why do Americans wear so much
padding when they play sports. All your games, you spend
more time dressing up than you do playing.

FLYNN

Basketball. Just a vest.

HENDERSON

Basketball is not a sport. Basketball is a freak show. The side
that breeds the tallest player wins. Also it's a girl's game, as is
baseball. You even pad up to play girls' games.

FLYNN

They're not your problem, Michael. The orphans. There's no
way you could do anything for them. They're not your
problem. You came here to report. That's all.

*He takes a long drag on the cigarette and then starts to splutter and
cough.*

CUT TO:

INT. BREAKFAST ROOM, HOLIDAY INN. DAY.

*Henderson joins Jane at a breakfast table. She is sitting with a
Frenchwoman, Nina.*

JANE

This is Nina.

NINA

Hello.

HENDERSON

Welcome to the fifteenth worst place on Earth.

NINA

Thank you.

JANE

She's an aid worker.

NINA

Children's charity. The Children's Embassy. We bought in food. We're taking out children. We've got a coach. I'm trying to pitch our story to your network.

HENDERSON

What sort of children?

NINA

I'm sorry?

HENDERSON

I mean . . . which children? What are you talking about?

NINA

I'm looking for children with relatives. In France and Italy. I can take babies too. Babies are easy to find homes for.

HENDERSON

I can get you babies tomorrow. Lots of babies. There's an orphanage. I know the people there. They're desperate. They're in the line of fire . . .

JANE

I thought you were leaving.

NINA

You could leave. You could leave on the coach with us. An epic story for you. The Exodus.

EXT. LJUBICA IVEZIC ORPHANAGE, SARAJEVO. DAY.

Mrs Savic embraces Henderson. Nina is cool. There are one or two co-workers with Nina.

> MRS SAVIC
> This is so wonderful. How have you done this?

> NINA
> It's what I came to do. I hope we will do it many times. From here though, I can only really take babies.

> MRS SAVIC
> The babies are the most important thing.

CUT TO:

INT. STAIRWAY, ORPHANAGE. DAY.

Mrs Savic is leading Henderson and Nina down into the cellar where the babies are kept. It is like one of the outer circles of the Inferno.

> NINA
> I can take five.

> MRS SAVIC
> I have nine. You choose.

INT. CELLAR, ORPHANAGE. DAY.

By this stage, they have reached the bottom of the stairs and Nina is confronted for the first time with the full horror of the filthy nursery. As always it takes her less than ten seconds to make up her mind.

> NINA
> I'll take them all.

> MRS SAVIC
> Thank you. You are a good woman.

> EMIRA *(in Bosnian, to Mrs Savic)*
> Is it true?

MRS SAVIC
(*Bosnian*)
Yes, it's true.

EMIRA
(*in Bosnian, to Mrs Savic*)
He's taking us out of here?

Nina relishes the happy look on Emira's face.

NINA
(*to Henderson*)
Someone is pleased.

MRS SAVIC
(*in Bosnian, to Emira*)
They are taking the babies. All the babies.

EMIRA
(*Bosnian*)
The babies? You're taking him without me?! You're taking
him away from me?!

*Emira starts to lose control. She is tearful and cross. She clutches the
Roadrunner baby.*

MRS SAVIC
(*Bosnian*)
It's for the best. Of course it is. If he can get out of here.

Emira pushes past Mrs Savic.

EMIRA
(*Bosnian*)
He promised. He promised me. He said he'd take me out of
here!

NINA
What's wrong?

*Mrs Savic is thrown by this. Emira is crying. Mrs Savic tries to take
the baby from her.*

MRS SAVIC
(*Bosnian*)
Give me the baby. You're scaring him.

Emira is like a fury now.

EMIRA
(*Bosnian*)
No! You can leave me here. But you can't take him away
from me. I won't let you take him.

Emira clutches the Roadrunner even more tightly. She runs away.

MRS SAVIC
She is saying Mr Henderson promised to take her out of here.

Nina looks at him. Henderson groans.

CUT TO:

INT. DORMITORIES, ORPHANAGE. DAY.

Mrs Savic and Nina are planning the evacuation of the babies.
Henderson is pleading with Nina.

HENDERSON
Couldn't you take her?

NINA
I can't. I can take babies and children with somewhere to go.
They're going for a rest. A holiday. Until the fighting is over.
They're not going to be adopted.

HENDERSON
She could come to my house. She could stay there.

Nina is taken aback. So is Mrs Savic. They stop what they are doing.

HENDERSON
Mrs Savic?

MRS SAVIC
(*to Henderson*)
You must ask Emira. It is her decision.

95

HENDERSON

I don't speak Bosnian.

CUT TO:

INT. LANDING, ORPHANAGE. DAY.

Emira is sitting quietly at the top of the stairs when Henderson comes up to her, accompanied by Mrs Savic. He looks up at Emira and starts to talk. Mrs Savic translates for him.

HENDERSON

It may be possible. It may be possible for you to come and stay with me. For a while at least. It will be difficult but it may be possible, if that's what you want.

Emira speaks to Mrs Savic, who talks to Henderson.

MRS SAVIC

She wants to know how long for. How long do you ask her for?

HENDERSON

I don't know. It's up to her.

MRS SAVIC

No. She's a child. She doesn't know. It's up to me. I brought her up.

HENDERSON

Of course.

MRS SAVIC

She belongs here with me.

HENDERSON

Yes. I realize that but . . .

MRS SAVIC

But these are dangerous times. One day, Mr Henderson, it will all be over and she will want to know where she belongs. Emira may go with you but you must bring her back soon. When the bombing is over.

96

Tell her.

Another conversation in Croatian between Mrs Savic and Emira.

Emira puts out her hands to Henderson. He shakes one awkwardly.

Till the bombing is over.

CUT TO:

EXT. STREETS, SARAJEVO. DAY.

Nina and Henderson are getting into the ITN minibus. Henderson will get in and start it up.

NINA

I don't want anyone to know. Not the driver. Not your news crew. You must not sit near her on the coach.

HENDERSON

Fine. Of course. I'm very grateful.

NINA

This is not legal. If they find out, they will charge you with kidnapping. You know that? Five years minimum.

HENDERSON

Yes. I realize that.

NINA

The Bosnian government is against evacuation. If you evacuate people, you're doing the Serbs work for them. If they find you out, I will say you lied to us. I will let them take you both prisoner.

HENDERSON

Good.

They have come to a Beware of the Sniper sign. Henderson slams his foot down on the accelerator and drives off.

Nina is taken aback by this response. She laughs.

CUT TO:

9 Roadrunner

INT. DORMITORY, ORPHANAGE. MORNING.

The big, spartan dormitory. Emira is asleep with Roadrunner, squashed into the little bed.

Mrs Savic is standing over the bed. She gently pushes the hair over Emira's forehead, out of her eyes. She goes to stroke her cheek but pulls back. She whispers Emira's name very quietly, as though saying, 'darling'. Then the child starts to stir and Mrs Savic says, 'EMIRA!' as though she were a sergeant major waking her for morning parade.

> MRS SAVIC
> (*Bosnian*)
> Wake up. You're late.

CUT TO:

INT. UNDERGROUND CAR PARK. DAY.

A big coach is parked up, waiting. Nina is sitting at a small trestle table with one of her co-workers, filling in forms. Mothers and children are queueing up at the trestle table, filling in forms, pleading, weeping, saying goodbye. The chaos of evacuation. The children are all wearing labels with their names on, like Second World War evacuees.

Pick up Greg filming this. Henderson talking to Flynn and Risto.

> FLYNN
> (*to Risto*)
> I'd like to apologize on behalf of the American people for our failure to deliver on the air strikes.

> RISTO
> Did you know that Pontius Pilate is revered as a Saint in the Serbian Orthodox Church?

> FLYNN
> Well he certainly came through for them this time.

Henderson is twitchy, looking around for some sign of Emira. Mothers are handing their children sandwiches.

Henderson spots Mrs Savic. She has come carrying a couple of babies. Other babies follow wheeled by her helpers and the older children. Henderson goes to help her. Henderson nods at her. She smiles back then gets on with the business of registering the babies. Slowly they filter onto the bus.

Henderson is on edge, looking round all the time for some sign of Emira. Then he spots her, carrying the Roadrunner. Henderson talks discreetly to Mrs Savic.

> HENDERSON
>
> Tell her not to talk to me. No one must know we're together.

Mrs Savic nods. Then starts to load her babies onto the bus. Emira comes and helps her. They work as a team, as they have done for years. When the last baby is on board, Mrs Savic tidies Emira's hair. She quickly gives Emira a photograph. It shows Mrs Savic and a baby.

> MRS SAVIC
> *(Bosnian)*
>
> It's you. And me. I think so anyway.
> *(light)*
> There have been so many.

Emira smiles. She looks at a mother weeping as her child goes.

> She is worried that by the time the child comes home she will be dead. You don't have that worry. No one will kill me.

Emira hugs her with sudden passion, then gets on the bus.

CUT TO:

INT. CONVOY BUS. DAY.

Nina is directing operations. People are shuffling babies and children around the bus.

> NINA
>
> I don't want the Muslims to sit together. Or the Serb babies.

If anyone gets on to inspect, it must look like babies, not Serb babies, not Muslim babies . . .

As she is saying this, Emira passes her with the Roadrunner. They exchange brief smiles.

                    (*to* Mrs Savic)
The baby with the Roadrunner. Is he Croat?

                    MRS SAVIC
Serb.

She gets onto the bus.

CUT TO:

EXT. BUS, UNDERGROUND CAR PARK. DAY.

Emira appears in the window, her back to the shelter. Mrs Savic reaches up and touches the window, where Emira's hair is leaning against it. Then she goes. Henderson spots her leaving and goes to speak to her but he is intercepted by a UN Official.

                    OFFICIAL
I'm sorry about this. There's been a bit of a hitch. We can't guarantee the ceasefire just yet.

                    HENDERSON
What? But . . .

                    OFFICIAL
But we'll try our best to do so as soon as possible. I can't let you take out a busload of children without some sort of cover. So . . . leave it with us. We'll be in touch.

He goes. Henderson looks at Nina.

                    NINA
Your phone will work down here?

                    HENDERSON
I think so.

                    NINA
I hope so.

INT. BUS, UNDERGROUND CAR PARK. EVENING.

It is getting dark. People are lighting candles. Some children are asleep. Some are crying. Emira is cradling Roadrunner. Henderson is with Nina. They are both looking at the phone.

NINA

You're sure it works?

HENDERSON

If it doesn't they'll send someone. Relax.

He goes back down the bus. Emira looks up at him. He winks and makes a 'shush' sign with his finger, then almost jumps out of his skin. The phone has rung. It keeps ringing. The sound is piercing in the silence of the underground.

NINA

I don't know how it works.

Henderson dashes down the bus to take it from her. Presses the right buttons. Nina talks into it in French. Then hangs up, again with Henderson's help.

NINA

We can go.

HENDERSON

Thank God.

NINA

We don't have two hours. Only one.

HENDERSON

Let's go.

CUT TO:

EXT. ROOF-TOPS, SARAJEVO. EVENING.

A UN armoured car leads the bus out of the underground car park. Pull focus to find that we are watching this from the point of view of two roof-top snipers. One of them has a mobile phone. He makes a call.

CUT TO:

EXT. STREETS, SARAJEVO. EVENING.

The bus moving along the rubble-strewn streets. It moves painfully slowly, having to edge its way round pot-holes and burnt-out cars.

CUT TO:

EXT. JUNCTION, STREETS, SARAJEVO. EVENING.

Pick up bus at a junction. The UN car in front has stopped. It starts to back up. The passenger waves the coach driver to do the same. The coach starts slowly to back up. Henderson jumps out and asks the Official:

HENDERSON

What's going on?

OFFICIAL

We could only guarantee a particular route. The Bosnian government doesn't really approve of evacuation. It is seen as giving the Serbs what they want. We have to go by the book. This has to be a special case.

CUT TO:

EXT. STREETS, SARAJEVO. EVENING.

The UN car moves down a much narrower street. The coach follows. It is extremely difficult. The coach barely fits. Eventually two UN officials jump out and start moving bins and bikes and so on to make more room for the coach as it edges along.

CUT TO:

EXT. ROOF-TOPS/STREETS, SARAJEVO. EVENING.

Pick up on two more armed men watching this from a nearby roof. One of them checks his watch, grins and makes a joke. The other one laughs.

CUT TO:

EXT. STREETS, SARAJEVO. EVENING.

Henderson has got out of the bus and is now helping clear rubbish and bikes himself.

CUT TO:

EXT. JUNCTION, STREETS, SARAJEVO. EVENING.

The bus emerges from the narrow street onto a much broader road and begins to pick up speed.

CUT TO:

EXT. CHECKPOINT/STREETS, SARAJEVO. EVENING.

They have stopped at a Serb checkpoint. The soldiers look menacing. The UN officials are remonstrating with them. Greg gets out to film what is happening. When the soldiers see the camera, they start shouting and cursing and telling him to stop. Greg gets back on the bus.

CUT TO:

INT. BUS, CHECKPOINT/STREETS. EVENING.

Greg goes to Henderson who is standing in the aisle next to Emira's seat.

GREG

They're mean-looking machines those FN-762s. I prefer them with the wooden butt. It looks more classical.

HENDERSON

Greg. Would you shut the fuck up?

Greg is taken aback.

The UN Official gets onto the bus and explains the situation.

OFFICIAL

They're insisting on searching the bus. I'm sorry about this. Everybody off.

The Co-worker translates this. The children are obviously frightened by it. They start, reluctantly, to move off the bus.

CUT TO:

EXT. CHECKPOINT/STREETS, SARAJEVO. EVENING.

Henderson watches Emira, carrying the roadrunner. As she is getting off the bus, he offers her his hand.

                          EMIRA
Thank you.

                          HENDERSON
English. Very good. Dobra.

She walks off to join the group.

CUT TO:

EXT. ROOF-TOPS/STREETS, SARAJEVO. EVENING.

We see the children and their escorts filing off the bus onto the street. Some of them looking anxiously up at the roof-tops.

Full focus to find that they have reason to be anxious. We have been watching this from the point of view of two snipers.

CUT TO:

EXT. CHECKPOINT/STREETS, SARAJEVO. EVENING.

The children stand around while the Serb soldiers go through the bus. Henderson and Nina keep looking at their watches. The deadline is getting close.

The soldiers wave them back onto the bus. Nina is panicky now. She hurries them on. The children dash and hurry. They bump into each other. There are more tears. The bus starts up and moves off.

CUT TO:

EXT. EDGE OF SARAJEVO. EVENING.

The bus passes under a bridge.

CUT TO:

INT. BUS, EDGE OF SARAJEVO. EVENING.

The Co-worker shouts something in Croatian and everyone cheers.

>   CO-WORKER
>   (*to Henderson*)
> That's it. We're out.

Henderson's face floods with relief. He is aware that the children are all laughing. They are looking at something out of the window.

CUT TO:

EXT. BUS, EDGE OF SARAJEVO. EVENING.

It is a madman, with no clothes on but covered with dirt, his long hair matted with filth, dancing around in a garden, waving at the bus.

CUT TO:

INT. BUS, EDGE OF SARAJEVO. EVENING.

Henderson watches until he is out of sight. As though it were some kind of bizarre blessing.

INT. BUS. COUNTRY ROADS. EVENING.

The bus ploughs on towards the mountains. The children all start singing, a skipping song maybe. Something cheerful and upbeat.

CUT TO:

EXT. MOUNTAIN ROADS. EVENING.

The bus is winding its way down difficult mountain roads. Night is falling. On the bus the children are asleep.

It keeps on driving into the night.

CUT TO:

EXT. MOUNTAIN ROADS. NIGHT.

The bus is now moving through difficult mountain roads. Pick up on it moving slowly with one tyre balanced on the edge. Greg is lighting the road with his camera lights.

The bus just about gets round the bend.

CUT TO:

EXT. MOUNTAIN ROADS. NIGHT.

The bus steams on for a while. Then comes another pass. The bus stops.

CUT TO:

EXT. MOUNTAIN FARM/VILLAGE. NIGHT.

Nina is talking to the UN Official.

NINA
My driver thinks it's not safe to try these roads in the dark.

OFFICIAL
Nothing's safe out here, Miss.

NINA
We will sleep here a few hours.

CUT TO:

EXT. MOUNTAIN FARM/VILLAGE. NIGHT.

Later Greg gets the light from his camera kit and sweeps the area. It is a farm.

CUT TO:

EXT. MOUNTAIN FARM/VILLAGE. NIGHT.

Campfires are built.

CUT TO:

EXT. MOUNTAIN FARM/VILLAGE. NIGHT.

Food is bought out for cooking. Someone starts to sing. The children are sitting round the fires, cooking sausages. An atmosphere of Summer Camp. Suddenly they are all singing. It is a magical, beautiful moment.

Greg is trying to film it but it is too dark. He points his Sun Gun into the trees. Emira is sitting underneath a tree with the Roadrunner. Henderson goes over to her. She is rocking the baby. He starts to sing 'Rock-a-bye Baby' while she rocks the baby back and forth. After a while, Emira tries to join in.

EMIRA

Tree top.

HENDERSON

Tree top. See. Tree. Top. Tree top.

He is pointing to a tree as he says this.

He takes out a photograph of his garden and shows it to her.

Garden. Garden. Tree. See? Tree. Trees.

Greg comes over.

GREG

You'd be better off teaching her Italian. That's where she's going isn't it?

HENDERSON

Do you *know* any Italian?

Pick up on the Driver, who is talking to Nina.

CUT TO:

EXT. MOUNTAIN FARM/VILLAGE. NIGHT.

Pick up on Nina and the Co-worker distributing cups of water and telling everyone not to wander off in case of mines.

CUT TO:

III

EXT. MOUNTAIN FARM/VILLAGE. NIGHT.

Emira rolls over on her side. She seems to be asleep. Henderson drapes his coat over her and carries her back onto the bus.

Henderson lies her down tenderly on a seat.

He goes back outside and sits down under the tree. Nina comes over to him.

> HENDERSON

Are you OK?

> NINA

Of course. So long as I don't make a single mistake, we have made it.

CUT TO:

INT. MRS SAVIC'S OFFICE, ORPHANAGE. NIGHT.

Mrs Savic is in her office. She looks up at the photographs of all the children on the wall.

She finds a recent one of Emira and with the tip of her finger, caresses the hair of the girl in the picture.

CUT TO:

EXT. MOUNTAIN FARM/VILLAGE. MORNING.

Henderson lying on his side, watching the sun come up over the hills. He looks up into the tree. The blossom is beautiful. He sits up and looks into the orchard.

There is something strange in one of the trees.

The decomposed body of a man is hanging there.

What's happened?

He runs to the bus.

CUT TO:

EXT. MOUNTAIN FARM/VILLAGE. MORNING.

UN Officials and Nina hurrying the children onto the bus.

> OFFICIAL
>
> It's a warning. We'd better get out.

CUT TO:

EXT. MOUNTAIN FARM/VILLAGE. MORNING.

Greg and Henderson filming in the village, which is as spookily quiet as a disused film set. The mosques are destroyed. Houses burnt out.

> GREG
>
> Look, that graffiti.

He starts to film the word ZIVKO *where it is daubed on a wall.*

CUT TO:

EXT. MOUNTAIN FARM/VILLAGE. DAY.

The bus is moving off.

EXT. BOSNIAN COUNTRYSIDE. DAY.

At the edge of a mountain pass, the UN officials shake hands with everyone and wish them luck. The bus moves on. The personnel carrier waits and watches until they are out of sight.

CUT TO:

EXT. FLAT ROADS, BOSNIAN COUNTRYSIDE. DAY.

Images of the bus worming its way through the mountains. Sometimes it moves quickly along the flat.

CUT TO:

EXT. HAIRPIN BEND, BOSNIAN COUNTRYSIDE. DAY.

At other times Henderson has to get out and guide the bus round hairpin bends. Greg films this.

CUT TO:

EXT. STEEP RISE, BOSNIAN COUNTRYSIDE. DAY.

In one place, the bus is stuck at the top of a steep rise. Everyone gets out and pushes it. When it makes it over the top, they all cheer.

CUT TO:

INT. BUS, BOSNIAN MOUNTAINS. DAY.

Henderson, Emira and the Roadrunner are sharing a seat on the coach. He keeps pointing things out as they pass and saying their names in English.

                    HENDERSON
Trees. Clouds. Grass. Coach. Seat.
                    (*etc.*)

Emira does not react at all. She is absorbed in the Roadrunner.

CUT TO:

INT. BUS, BOSNIAN COUNTRYSIDE. DAY.

The bus is bowling along. The children are singing, playing, shouting, making a huge racket. Henderson, Emira and the Roadrunner are together again. Henderson is drawing a face on a paper handkerchief. He stretches the tissue over his hand to make a simple puppet.

CUT TO:

INT./EXT. BUS. BOSNIAN COUNTRYSIDE. DAY.

Suddenly, the bus brakes very hard indeed, sending children sliding off their seats. Some of them giggle.

Nina follows the driver's gaze and there, up ahead of them, a posse of dark figures looms into the road and stops.

A couple of motorbikes, a jeep, a bristling plenitude of assault weaponry. Chetniks. Nina's face falls.

                    NINA
Chetniks. Drive on. Slowly.

The bus starts to edge forward.

114

Henderson bites his lip. He gets up from his seat at the back and moves down to sit next to Emira and the Roadrunner.

CUT TO:

EXT. BUS. BOSNIAN COUNTRYSIDE. DAY.

The Chetnik Leader smiles a huge smile then takes his gun from his back and levels it at the bus. The bus stops. The Chetnik Leader climbs casually onto the bus.

CUT TO:

INT. BUS, MOUNTAINS. DAY.

The Chetnik Leader addresses the Driver; a Co-worker translates to Nina.

Henderson is sitting next to Emira now. The Co-worker is behind them.

The Chetnik Leader asks if there are any 'Balija' on the bus (this is a derogative term for Muslims).

> NINA
> Tell him no. We have no Muslim children on this bus.

Pick up on the Muslim children quaking in their seats. The Chetnik Leader shrugs and keeps looking. Finally, he points to one child.

> CHETNIK LEADER
> (*Bosnian*)
> This one.

> NINA
> He's not Muslim. Serb. Serb. We have no Muslim children.

> CHETNIK LEADER
> (*Bosnian*)
> I know. I want Serb children. It's not patriotic for Serb children to leave Greater Serbia. They should stay. They should help build our new Fatherland.

Nina is aghast. Henderson hasn't understood a word.

HENDERSON
What's going on?

NINA
Just sit still. Everybody sit still.

The Chetnik Leader is checking the children's name labels. Swiftly Henderson rips Emira's off her blouse and slips it into his pocket.

The Chetnik Leader has come across Greg and his cameras. He insists on being filmed. He poses with his rifle while Greg shoots some footage of him. He is delighted by this.

Then suddenly he swings round and points to three children, sends them off the bus. This includes the Serb girl who told the joke earlier. Nina wants to say something but can't.

The Chetnik Leader comes and stares at Emira. He points to her blouse and asks where her label is.

HENDERSON
She's with me. She's English.

The Chetnik Leader doesn't understand. Nina comes and takes the label out of Henderson's pocket. She points to it.

NINA

Croat. Look. Croat. Not Serb.

The Chetnik Leader snarls, then moves on a little way. Emira and Henderson seem briefly relieved. Then the Chetnik Leader turns round and casually picks up the Roadrunner from where he is sleeping on the next seat. He handles the baby as though it is a bag of shopping. Emira jumps up from her seat but Henderson blocks her with his arm.

The Chetnik Leader reads the label on Roadrunner. It's a Serb name. He tucks the baby under his arm and goes. He walks down the bus in an envelope of silence.

Emira's body is rigid with horror, hatred and anger. She jumps up in her seat and stands in the aisle. Then she freezes there.

Some other children start to cry and protest. Nina yells at them.

NINA

Be quiet! All of you! Sit down! Be quiet!
(*to Driver*)
Tell them.

Sublimely indifferent, the Chetnik Leader climbs down from the bus.

The bus starts up. Emira turns round to find Henderson standing behind her. She lifts her arms up to him. Almost a gesture of surrender. He lifts her into his chest. She looks over his shoulder as the bus moves off.

The bus edges slowly past the Chetniks. We see the Chetnik Leader pass Roadrunner to a Motorbike Chetnik, who slings him casually under his arm.

The other children are herded onto the back of the jeep.

Emira keeps looking as long as she can.

The sight of the children in the custody of the Chetniks is blazed into her brain.

CUT TO:

INT. BUS, COUNTRYSIDE. DAY.

Emira is sitting next to Henderson, looking out of the window. They are passing through forest now. Suddenly, Emira speaks.

EMIRA
Trees.

Henderson is pleased, but knows better than to push it.

Clouds. Grass. Seat.

She says the same words in the same order that Henderson said them earlier.

He takes his photographs out again and shows her the one of the garden.

HENDERSON
Garden.

She says nothing but holds the picture up against the window of the bus. The real landscape rolls past behind the photograph. She starts to hum 'Rock-a-bye Baby'.

CUT TO:

INT. BUS. COUNTRYSIDE. DAY.

Pick up on Henderson sitting next to Nina.

HENDERSON
There wasn't anything we . . . you . . . could do.

NINA
(*rigid*)
Of course not. I expected to get forty out. I have nearly sixty. What are five babies more or less.

Henderson can see that it is only by a supreme effort that Nina can keep her feelings down.

CUT TO:

EXT. BUS, MOUNTAINS. DAY.

The bus moving through the mountains. It comes to a pass and there is a glint of blue, far below.

    CUT TO:

INT. BUS, NEAR THE SEA. DAY.

One of the children sees the sea. He shouts, in Bosnian, 'The sea! The sea!' They all jump over to that side of the coach and look at the sea.

    CUT TO:

EXT. BEACH. DAY.

The coach trundles onto a beach. The children all pour off the coach and run to the water.

Nina is helping the little ones down the high step of the big bus, onto the sand. Henderson is helping.

                NINA
Don't go into the water. Not too deep.
          (to Henderson)
I don't want them all to drown, now that we have finally made it.

Her eyes fill up with tears as she says these last two words. Henderson takes a step towards her but she waves him away.

No. I'm not going to cry. I'm not going to . . . fuck it, why not?

She starts to cry. He puts his arm around her. Henderson looks down the beach to where all the children are playing chicken. A row of babies, sitting just out of the waves' reach, makes a comic sight.

Greg is spinning Emira around in the air. He lets her down. She runs off to join her friends.

Henderson joins Greg.

                GREG
She's picked up quite a bit of English.

HENDERSON

Yeah. Well. Most important language in the world, you know.

Pick up on Nina, who has lined up all the children along the water's edge. They are staring at the horizon. Nina is pointing out to sea.

NINA

It's just over there. Italy. Not very far.

The children all start staring out to sea. Nina smiles indulgently.

You can't see it. It's too far. But not so far. There is no war there.

The children all stare intensely.

Come. Back to the bus.

But the children don't move.

CUT TO:

Pick up on all the children lined up next to the bus. Henderson is

counting heads, as is Nina. Most of the children are carrying babies, but not Emira.

> NINA
> Do we have all the babies?

> HENDERSON
> Fourteen.

> NINA
> *(pained, recalling the fifteenth)*
> Yes, fourteen.

They all file back onto the bus. Emira goes last.

CUT TO:

EXT. BUS, NEAR SEA/OUTSKIRTS OF SPLIT. DAY.

Bus entering Split and negotiating the streets of the town, heading for the harbour.

CUT TO:

EXT. HARBOUR, SPLIT. DAY.

The children are piling off the bus again. They are excited to be going on a boat. The boat is at the harbour. Nina, Greg and Henderson have great difficulty getting the children to line up and stay in line.

Henderson watches the babies go on board.

Nina spots Emira, bends down to her.

> NINA
> Good luck, Emira. I should say it in Bosnian –
> *(does so)*
> It may be a long time before you speak your own language again.

They take their leave of each other in Bosnian, then she runs away. Nina goes to Henderson and hugs him.

> Goodbye.

HENDERSON
Good luck.

NINA
People will tell you that bringing a child home will make no difference. Because they cannot imagine a political solution, they think there is no need to be a human. If everyone was a human, there would not be a political problem. You did a good thing. You did the right thing.

HENDERSON
Thank you.

As the gangplank is brought up, pick up on Greg who is standing next to Emira.

GREG
(*sanguine*)
So. You missed the boat, kid.

EMIRA
(*happily pointing at it*)
Boat!

Henderson comes up.

GREG
Missed the boat. What are we going to do?

HENDERSON
She'll have to come with us.

They turn and walk to the hotel.

GREG
Why didn't you say?

HENDERSON
I didn't want to compromise your journalistic integrity.

GREG
Oh. Right. Thanks.

They come to the front of the hotel. It is very exciting. Emira is delighted.

Here?

Henderson nods. She runs inside.

CUT TO:

INT. HOTEL, SPLIT. DAY.

Henderson walks into the room, dumps his bags on the floor, crosses to the window and looks out. From here he can see the ferry sailing away.

EXT. TERRACE, HOTEL, SPLIT. EVENING.

Greg, Henderson and Emira eating supper. Henderson is trying to teach Emira her new address. Emira keeps looking round at the fixtures and fittings excitedly.

EMIRA

Thirteen . . . Willawalk

HENDERSON

Will-ow. Willow. It's a kind of tree.

EMIRA

Tree?

HENDERSON

This kind. Look. A tree. Willow.

He draws a willow on the napkin.

GREG

She's going to think you live in a tree.

HENDERSON

Willow Walk. Thirteen Willow Walk.

He demonstrates walking using his fingers on the table. Emira gives up and points to Greg.

EMIRA

You.

GREG

What? My address? You're going to love this. Five . . .

She holds up five fingers.

Five. Very good. Number five, Druid's Bottom.

He points to his own bottom. She looks confused and then she starts to laugh.

CUT TO:

INT. HOTEL ROOM, SPLIT. EVENING.

INTERCUT WITH INT. HENDERSON'S HOUSE, ENGLAND. EVENING.

Emira is asleep on the bed. Henderson makes a phone call to Helen. As soon as the phone rings, we pick up on Helen, who is lying asleep in bed.

HENDERSON

Helen? Hi, it's me.

HELEN

Michael! I tried to ring you. Are you OK?

HENDERSON

I'm coming home.

HELEN

Oh. Good.

HENDERSON

I'm in Split. Remember? We came with the boys. I'm bringing someone with me.

HELEN

What?

HENDERSON

I'm bringing . . . a visitor. She's going to stay a while.

HELEN
(*sleepy*)

Not Greg?

124

HENDERSON

No. Not Greg. Go back to sleep. I'll see you tomorrow.

He looks down at the girl on the bed. He takes out his passport, which is bulging with exotic visas. He finds the back page and writes in 'Emira Henderson – Daughter'.

CUT TO:

EXT. BURNING HOUSE. DAY.

A house on fire. Tracer fire rakes the sky. A child comes running towards us out of the flames. It drops down in front of us. We are in one of Henderson's nightmares.

Another child comes out. This one lifts up its arms to Henderson. Just as he is about to lift the child, it gets shot and screams.

This is clearly happening in Bosnia.

The child screams and Henderson wakes up.

CUT TO:

INT. HOTEL ROOM, SPLIT. NIGHT.

Henderson sees that Emira on the other bed is screaming.

He jumps out of bed and goes to comfort her.

Shushes her. Picks her up. Carries her to the window and shows her what is outside – the sea.

CUT TO:

EXT. HOTEL. SPLIT. DAY.

Emira and Greg are playing by the hotel pool. Henderson comes over with a shopping bag full of stuff. He takes out a T-shirt with HI, EVERYBODY *written on it. He offers it to Emira.*

HENDERSON

You've got to wear this. I want people to think you're English. English. OK?

EMIRA
Druid bottom!

She kicks water at them and laughs. It turns into a full-scale water fight. She falls over. We go under the water with Emira.

Emira holds her breath and stays under the water for what seems like a very long time. Far away voices.

CUT TO:

EXT. SWIMMING POOL, LONDON. DAY.

Emira finally breaks the surface of the water. She is now in an outdoor swimming pool in London (Hampstead Heath Bathing Pond).

She looks around and sees Henderson sitting on a deck chair at the side of the pond. He is playing with his own two children. They are toddlers – Madeline (two) and Dominic (four). He hands Emira a towel.

CUT TO:

EXT. STREETS, LONDON. DAY.

Emira is holding Dominic's hand. Henderson and Helen are taking turns to push Madeline in her pushchair.

EMIRA
Heath Road South . . . then what?

Dominic thinks as he walks and hazards an answer.

DOMINIC
Home.

EMIRA
No, after Heath Road South, Keats Grove, Keats Grove Downshire Hill then . . .

DOMINIC
Pilgrim's Lane.

EMIRA
No. Home. Home.

DOMINIC

I'm cold.

CUT TO:

INT. THE HENDERSONS' LIVING ROOM. EVENING.

Dominic sits next to Emira on the couch, tucking into pizza. Emira is absorbed in the TV. A report on Sarajevo comes up. Henderson is in the room but not Helen.

EMIRA

That's where I live.

It doesn't look like much to brag about. The report continues. It starts to tell the story of Nina's second convoy, on which two babies were shot by snipers. It is very distressing. Helen comes into the room and spots it.

HELEN

Michael . . .

Henderson is absorbed.

Michael for goodness sake.

MICHAEL

Oh. Sorry.

He remembers the presence of the children. By now Helen has found the buttons.

HELEN

Let's see if we can find something more cheerful, shall we?

She channel flicks. The Loony Toons music comes on. The Roadrunner skids to a standstill in the middle of the screen, says 'Meep meep', and then Emira screams, a great howl of protest and inarticulate fear and loss. Henderson realizes immediately what has happened, scoops her into his arms and runs upstairs with her.

CUT TO:

INT. THE HENDERSONS' BEDROOM. EVENING.

Henderson sitting on the end of the bed, cradling Emira in his arms.

HENDERSON
Just cry. Just cry. Cry all you like.

CUT TO:

INT. THE HENDERSONS' KITCHEN. EVENING.

Helen sitting with Dominic.

HELEN
She gets upset. Because her home is so far away. You'd be upset, wouldn't you. If you lived far away.

DOMINIC
It's sad too. When the Coyote gets killed.

CUT TO:

10 Phone Home

INT. HOUSE. VILLAGE IN BOSNIA. DAY.

*An elderly man is putting on his best clothes. He adjusts his hat in the
mirror. He looks like a farmer dressed for some sort of fiesta. He is in
fact Emira's Uncle. He picks up a newspaper clipping from the table.
We see that it is illustrated with a photograph of Emira.*

    CUT TO:

EXT. BOSNIAN VILLAGE/COUNTRYSIDE. DAY.

*Uncle walking in his village. The countryside around is beautiful. An
idyllic scene. There should be a pretty mosque somewhere in shot.*

    CUT TO:

EXT. POLICE STATION. BOSNIAN VILLAGE. DAY.

Pick up Uncle in the village outside a police station. He goes inside.

    CUT TO:

INT. POLICE STATION. DAY.

*The Uncle talking in Croatian to the Policeman. He shows him the
clipping.*

    CUT TO:

INT. HOLIDAY INN. SARAJEVO. DAY.

*A Policeman walks into reception, asks a question of the Receptionist.
The Receptionist points out Jane. Policeman goes to Jane, talks to her
for a while and then pulls out a document with a photograph of Emira
on it.*

    CUT TO:

INT. HENDERSON'S KITCHEN. NIGHT.

Helen is working in the kitchen. The phone rings and she answers it.

HELEN

Michael! Phone!

Henderson comes in and answers the call. The date goes up.

AUGUST 1993

HENDERSON

Flynn!

(*to Helen*)

It's Flynn!

HELEN

I know.

HENDERSON

Are you still there? How d'you get a call out?

CUT TO:

INT. THE HENDERSONS' KITCHEN. NIGHT.

INTERCUT WITH INT. HOLIDAY INN. NIGHT.

Flynn is on the phone, with Jane standing next to him. In a moment, there will be some difficult news and Jane will lean on Flynn.

FLYNN

We've got our own satellite phone now. I blagged the network. I sell phone calls on the side. Jane wants to talk to you.

HENDERSON

Great.

Jane takes the phone.

JANE

How's the kid?

132

HENDERSON

Good. Complicated but good.

JANE

She want to come back?

HENDERSON

No of course not. I told Mrs Savic not until the bombing stops.

JANE

The thing is . . . that someone wants her to come back.

HENDERSON

Someone like who?

(*to Emira*)

Emira, go to bed.

JANE

Like . . . Emira's mother. Her uncle contacted us here. Emira has a mother, Michael. She wants her back.

End the scene on Flynn and Jane in Sarajevo.

CUT TO:

STOCK FOOTAGE. EXT. HOLIDAY INN, SARAJEVO. NIGHT.

The city being shelled from the point of view of the hotel.

CUT TO:

INT. HENDERSON'S KITCHEN. MORNING.

Henderson, Helen and Emira are all sitting around the table. They are telling her the news.

HELEN

Do you have friends at home? Do you miss them a lot?

EMIRA

Did the bombing stopped?

Henderson and Helen both shake their heads.

133

No. Not yet.

EMIRA

So, I stay here.

She looks from one to the other. It's all so simple.

What? What happened?

HENDERSON

Your mother, Emira. Your mother has . . . made contact . . .
spoken. To us.

EMIRA

My mother?

This is totally bewildering. She tries to take it in.

My mother. She rang here? This house?

HENDERSON

Not exactly. She wants you back, Emira.

Helen reaches out and holds Emira's hand across the table.

EMIRA

I must go back?

HENDERSON

She wants you back.

Emira thinks, then shakes her head.

EMIRA

No. It is too late.

HENDERSON

You did not come here for ever. I promised Mrs Savic to
bring you back after the bombing had stopped.

EMIRA

It has not stopped.

HENDERSON

No. No it hasn't. But you don't belong to us.

                              EMIRA

I belong to me.

                            HENDERSON

No. You don't. I know it sounds strange but you don't. She is
your mother.

                              EMIRA

I don't want her to be my mother. I want you to be my
mother. Don't you want to be my mother?

Helen looks at Henderson.

                              HELEN

Yes. Yes I do.

CUT TO:

INT. HENDERSON'S BEDROOM. NIGHT.

Henderson and Helen are lying in bed. He is staring at the ceiling.

                            HENDERSON

How was I supposed to know she had a mother? She was in
an orphanage, for Christ's sake.

                              HELEN

Sssssh.

                            HENDERSON

Sorry. Go to sleep.

There's a pause. He carries on staring at the ceiling.

                              HELEN

You're going to have to go back there.

                            HENDERSON

I know.

                              HELEN

You'll have to find the mother and explain to her. Tell her
we'll adopt Emira.

                            HENDERSON

And if she says no?

                               135

HELEN

I don't know.

HENDERSON

And if I can't find her?

HELEN

I don't know.

HENDERSON

Well neither do I.

11   This is the End

INT. THE HENDERSONS' HOUSE, ENGLAND. MORNING.

Henderson is in the children's bedroom. Emira is in a single bed. The other two share a double. There are mobiles and toys all over the place. He kisses his own two children and stands looking down at Emira. Helen appears behind him in her dressing gown. She leans on him.

> HENDERSON
> Wonder if I should wake her up.

> HELEN
> No. I want you to myself.

She leads him out.

CUT TO:

EXT. THE HENDERSONS' HOUSE. MORNING.

A taxi pulls up. A cold, early-morning feel. The light is on in the Hendersons' doorway. The door opens and Henderson appears, with Helen behind him. He turns and gives her a brisk kiss.

> HELEN
> Take care.

He jumps into the cab and waves as it pulls off. As it moves away, Emira appears in the doorway next to Helen. Too late to wave.

CUT TO:

INT. HOLIDAY INN, SARAJEVO. NIGHT.

A rock band is cranking out 'Eve of Destruction' at one end of the heavily sandbagged ballroom. A parade of girls in swimsuits makes its way across the stage. They are all wearing numbers on their wrists. They wave and wiggle. The crowd goes crazy. The MC winds up the crowd. He speaks in Croatian. However, the words, 'Miss Besieged Sarajevo' comes over clearly. He repeats them over and over.

139

Someone taps Henderson on the shoulder and he spins around to be confronted by Flynn.

FLYNN
Welcome to Hell.

HENDERSON
Did you ever try to get another job, Flynn?

FLYNN
I'm covering the Miss World contest, starting with the Sarajevo heats.

Someone hugs Henderson. It is Jane, then Annie.

ANNIE
It's brilliant to see you.

HENDERSON
Wasn't sure how welcome I'd be.

JANE
If we ever get out of here, we're all going to take a kid back.

HENDERSON

Thank you. You know, I have to find the mother . . .

JANE

It's going to be fine. I've got some good news.

HENDERSON

What?

JANE

The uncle. The one who made the phone call. He's here. In
Sarajevo. You can go and see him tomorrow. So that's a bit of
luck. His village was ethnically cleansed. Oh. God that was a
terrible thing to say, wasn't it?

HENDERSON

Yes, it was.

Flynn suddenly shushes everyone.

FLYNN

Jesus, look at this.

*In the corner of the lobby, is a big TV screen, geared to a news channel.
Our characters start to watch it and a huge crowd gathers around them.
Even the band stops playing.*

*The Newsreader (Djogo) has just finished reading the news. Instead of
signing off, he has pulled a gun, and is holding it to his own head and
yelling. As they watch, he pulls the trigger. There is a loud explosion, a
splash of blood across the screen and he drops out of sight.*

*Nothing happens on the TV for a moment. Henderson, Flynn, Annie
and Jane stare in silence at the silent screen. The tension is palpable and
lasts for some time.*

*Then the Newsreader pops back up, wipes away the fake blood and
starts to rant.*

HENDERSON

What did he say!

FLYNN

Same old thing.

ANNIE
The whole place has gone crazy.

CUT TO:

EXT./INT. UNDERGROUND CAR PARK, HOLIDAY INN. DAY.

Jane is showing Henderson their new car – it's an armoured Land-Rover. She shows him a row of bullet holes along the side.

JANE
It's from Northern Ireland. We got these last week in Dobrinja . . . this one we picked up this morning in the road you are about to visit.

HENDERSON
Thanks.

She hands Henderson a roughly drawn map.

JANE
You should be all right in this. There's a Muslim checkpoint just here. But you should be OK. I spoke to someone there yesterday so just mention my name. Don't forget.

He gets in.

CUT TO:

EXT. ENTRANCE TO CAR PARK, HOLIDAY INN. DAY.

Land-Rover leaves car park.

EXT. STREETS, SARAJEVO. DAY.

Henderson driving along a city street. He checks the napkin map on his passenger seat. Up ahead, he sees the road-block – a makeshift collection of huts.

CUT TO:

EXT. CHECKPOINT, STREETS, SARAJEVO. DAY.

Henderson pulls up. A soldier walks towards him. The soldier is not in any complete uniform. His weapon is elderly. He is obviously a member of some sort of local militia. He orders Henderson out.

HENDERSON

I was sent by Carson. Jane Carson.

It doesn't seem to mean much to the soldier.

The soldier starts to guide Henderson towards the makeshift checkpoint hut. Henderson keeps saying Jane's name to the soldier and the soldier seems to be agreeing with him. He takes an increasingly nervous Henderson to the hut. He has to stoop to get inside.

CUT TO:

INT. CHECKPOINT HUT. DAY.

Henderson's eyes take a while to get accustomed to the gloom. When they do he sees a figure standing in the gloom. The figure comes slowly towards him. It is Risto.

HENDERSON

Risto.

Risto smiles and embraces Henderson.

RISTO

Welcome to Hell.

HENDERSON

You joined up.

RISTO

The Serbs were making such a racket. It was bringing down the whole neighbourhood. I decided I had to do something about it. I have to say I expected something more dashing in the way of a uniform.

HENDERSON

I can't imagine it.

RISTO

Anyway, I can't wear it where we're going.

He starts to take off his uniform.

143

CUT TO:

EXT. STREETS, SARAJEVO. DAY.

They are driving through badly bomb-damaged streets.

> HENDERSON
> Hey. I got you some Jammy Dodgers. They're in the bag.
> There. On the floor.

> RISTO
> Fantastic.
> *(gets them)*
> I've started to get cravings. It's like being pregnant. This week
> it's dental floss. I never flossed my teeth in my life. But I want
> some floss now. Last week I think it was peaches. And before
> that, warmth.

> HENDERSON
> You haven't changed.

> RISTO
> Yes I have. I have lost my innocence.

144

HENDERSON

I don't remember you having innocence.

RISTO

I used to think my life and the siege were different things.
Now I realize there is no life in Sarajevo apart from the siege.
The siege is Sarajevo. If you are not part of it you are asleep.
So. Now I have lost my innocence.

HENDERSON

You're trying to tell me you killed someone.

RISTO
(*looking out of the window*)
Yes. It was not so bad. Therapeutic.

CUT TO:

EXT. BLOCK OF FLATS, SARAJEVO. DAY.

Risto and Henderson come to a particular block of flats and pause.

RISTO

We're here.

The Land-Rover pulls up. Henderson and Risto get out of the Land-Rover. Henderson looks at the door a long time, takes a deep breath and then knocks.

CUT TO:

INT. BLOCK OF FLATS, SARAJEVO. DAY.

The Uncle we saw earlier is now in his best clothes. He shakes Henderson's hand enthusiastically. Henderson glances round the gloomy, spartan room and sees the press cutting of Emira pinned to the wall. The room is full of other refugees, each of whom has made a kind of nest of bags and boxes in a corner. There are mattresses everywhere. There is a moment of pause, as of some etiquette unfulfilled. Henderson takes out a packet of cigarettes, a set of batteries and a tube of toothpaste. The Uncle's eyes are almost damp with rapture. The other refugees stare as discreetly as possible. The Uncle says something to Risto, goes to the corner, takes a jug of water and starts to brush his teeth with the toothpaste. Henderson and Risto wait.

The Uncle sits down and starts to talk very seriously and intently to Henderson in Bosnian. Henderson looks at Risto for help.

> RISTO
> Milicia – that's her mother's name.

The Uncle nods vigorously. Milicia is the mother's name. Then he starts to root in some plastic bags.

> He's looking for photographs. He keeps apologizing for the mess. The Fascists, the Croats, they came to his village. He had to pack in a hurry.

Pick up on the Uncle who has found some photographs. He looks at them in the palm of his hand.

CUT TO:

INT./EXT. HOUSE, UNCLE'S VILLAGE. DAY.

The same photographs arranged on a shelf. The Uncle is hurriedly sweeping them into the plastic bag we saw in the previous scene. He dashes to the window and peeps out. Some big four-wheel drives are pulling up outside. A man in paramilitary uniform steps out and looks around. This is Zivko.

CUT TO:

INT. UNCLE'S BLOCK OF FLATS, SARAJEVO. DAY.

The Uncle still staring abstractedly at the photographs in his hand.

> RISTO
> (*Bosnian*)
> Did you find them?

> UNCLE
> (*Bosnian*)
> Yes, yes.

With a big smile, he hands over the photographs to Henderson and Risto.

RISTO
(*to Henderson*)
These are of Emira's Mother.

HENDERSON
She's the image of Emira.

UNCLE
(*English*)
Emira no. Milicia.

HENDERSON
Yes. They're alike. Very alike.
(*to Risto*)
I don't want to know all this. I just want to know where she is.

He fans out the photographs. Milicia is standing in a bewildering variety of different places. Risto asks the question. The Uncle misunderstands and starts to explain where each photograph was taken – Budapest, Belgrade, etc. Risto tries again.

RISTO
But now? Where does she live now?

Someone comes in through the main door of the house. Daylight bursts into the room. From the Uncle's POV we see:

INT. UNCLE'S HOUSE, VILLAGE. DAY.

A Croat paramilitary bursts in through the door. The Uncle is about to scurry out the back way with his plastic bags. The paramilitary yells at him and bundles him out of the front door.

CUT TO:

INT. UNCLE'S BLOCK OF FLATS, SARAJEVO. DAY.

Risto is talking, still trying to get through to the Uncle, whom he believes to be simply preoccupied.

RISTO
But could you tell us where she lives now.

The Uncle looks up.

UNCLE
(*Bosnian*)
She has lost many things. We have all lost many things. You
must understand. If there is a chance of getting something
back. Anything. You must understand that we will take that
chance. Just to have something that belongs to us.

RISTO
(*Bosnian*)
Of course.

(*English*)
I don't think he's going to give it to us. Oh –

The Uncle starts writing down the address.

This is it. It's in Sarajevo.
(*Bosnian*)
Good. Thank you.

*Henderson takes the piece of paper eagerly and pumps the Uncle's hand.
Henderson and Risto leave. We stay on the Uncle, who sits alone and
apart in the smoky hubbub of the house.*

CUT TO:

EXT. UNCLE'S VILLAGE. DAY.

*A lovely day, a lovely village. Quiet and rustic. A fashionable Japanese
four-wheel drive pulls up. Zivko gets out and takes a breath of air. It is
the same moment we saw earlier from the POV of the Uncle's house.*

We see the Uncle looking fearfully out of the window of his house.

CUT TO:

INT. UNCLE'S HOUSE, VILLAGE. DAY.

*The Uncle desperately packing the established photographs. He hurries
for the back door but the front door bursts open, as we have already
seen, and a Croat Paramilitary bursts in and grabs the Uncle.*

CUT TO:

EXT./INT. UNCLE'S VILLAGE. DAY.

Several old people are being herded onto the back of a big lorry. The old Uncle is among them.

They watch in horror as Zivko and some sidekicks lead a group of young village men towards a tall building. The young men are tied together.

Meanwhile, neighbours appear in doorways and look calmly on. A Paramilitary jokes with one of them.

INT. STAIRWAY. VILLAGE. DAY.

The young men keep going up the stairs, falling from time to time. Eventually, they come out onto the roof of the flats.

   CUT TO:

EXT. ROOF, MUSLIM FLATS. DAY.

Zivko watches the young Muslim men being brought out onto the roof. His friend follows them out and goes to join the man with his back to us.

There is shouting in Bosnian and the young men back up towards the edge of the roof.

Zivko produces his gun. He aims and shoots the young man at the very end of the line.

The young man falls backwards off the roof, almost dragging the others off after him. They strain and haul on the line, trying to keep them falling off the roof.

The dead man dangles from the rope attached to the other prisoners.

Zivko aims, fires again. This time it is much harder for the five remaining prisoners to take the weight. But they manage it.

Now Zivko shoots the man at the other end of the line so that the prisoners are pulled both ways.

Now Zivko is truly delighted at the agony and the fear on the faces of the prisoners.

ZIVKO
(*calmly; in Serbian*)
My name is Zivko.

Shoots another prisoner.

I believe in God.

And now they all fall off the edge of the roof. Zivko goes to the edge himself, intending to fire down into the pile of bodies.

And God believes in me.

We look down with Zivko and realize that there are far more than seven bodies down there. Maybe thirty or more. A little way off, two soldiers are painting the name Zivko on the gable wall.

CUT TO:

INT. ITN LAND-ROVER, STREETS, SARAJEVO. DAY.

Henderson and Risto drive through Sarajevo. The Land-Rover slows up. They are coming to a heavily bombed area.

HENDERSON
Is that it?

CUT TO:

EXT. BOMBED HOUSES, SARAJEVO (DORINJA). DAY.

There doesn't seem to be a single building left standing. Henderson and Risto get out and walk into the bombed area. They stop a child who is running by.

RISTO
Number seventeen?

The child points to a heap of rubble. They look around. No sign of anything.

RISTO
Maybe she's dead. Maybe you can just go home and forget it.

Henderson shakes his head.

HENDERSON

I have to know, Risto. I have to make her safe.

RISTO

Are you ready to play Sarajevo's favourite game?

HENDERSON

What?

RISTO

It's called, Is There A God?

They look at each other, lower their heads and run like maniacs towards the houses.

CUT TO:

EXT. HOUSE, SARAJEVO. DAY.

Henderson and Risto make their way towards one of the houses. Faces appear at them from windows.

RISTO

Well is there?

HENDERSON

I'll tell you when I get that signature.
(*beat*)
Is this where they want her to live?

CUT TO:

EXT. HOUSE, SARAJEVO. DAY.

Pick them up stopping at a front door. Risto knocks at a door. An old woman looks out. He starts to question her in Croatian but there is no response.

He tries the next door. No response at all.

The next door, a young woman answers. About ten people look anxiously out of the house behind her.

Once again Risto gets no sense out of her.

*They turn to go on when they are hailed from behind by a young man,
who beckons to them.*

They hesitate. He talks urgently.

RISTO
He says he knows what we are looking for.

*Henderson and Risto exchange glances. Then they set out after the
young man.*

*Faces appear in doorways. They follow him, looking around all the
time. The tension is palpable. They follow him to a doorway. The young
man shouts through the letter-box. Henderson and Risto look at each
other.*

HENDERSON
Is this it? Is she in there?

RISTO
He says he's got what we're looking for.

*A woman comes to the door. The young man talks to her, smiles at
Risto and Henderson. The woman goes inside.*

HENDERSON
Is this it? Is that her? Is that her mother?

RISTO
I don't think we should go in here.

HENDERSON
What?

RISTO
I don't know these people. I don't know who they are. Come
on. I think we should go.

HENDERSON
I'm going in.

RISTO
Don't. Come on.

HENDERSON
I've got to.

Risto has grabbed Henderson's sleeve. Henderson shoves him off.

I've got to.

He goes inside.

CUT TO:

INT. HALLWAY, HOUSE, SARAJEVO. DAY.

Henderson goes into the house. It's dark and disorientating. Unfamiliar faces stare at Henderson. Upstairs, someone is shouting angrily. The young man reappears, beckoning him onwards. Henderson looks back and sees that Risto has followed him. Henderson goes on into the main room.

CUT TO:

INT. MAIN ROOM, HOUSE, SARAJEVO. DAY.

The room is full of people, hard-looking people, all staring at him. An air of secrecy and tension. Henderson does not know where to look. Is one of these people Emira's mother? Suddenly, the young man is holding a toilet roll and more or less shoving it in Henderson's face. He is obviously imploring him to feel the quality.

RISTO
He wants you to buy it. Look. The place is full of stuff.

Indeed, the room is like a warehouse, piled with toilet rolls and bags of flour with 'UN' printed on the side.

Henderson holds his hands up in refusal.

HENDERSON
Tell him there's been a misunderstanding.

Risto tries to explain. The two start to back away. The young man becomes very very aggressive. He starts to bawl at Henderson, as though insulted. Henderson and Risto keep trying to back out. Suddenly, they are grabbed from behind and pulled out onto the street.

CUT TO:

EXT. HOUSE, SARAJEVO. DAY.

Two heavies are forcing Henderson and Risto against a wall. The young man is now bawling at them to search the strangers' pockets. He is clearly terrified of them.

RISTO

He thinks we're police. He thinks we've got guns.

He tries to remonstrate in Bosnian. It is a nervy, edgy scene. The heavies find three boxes of Marlboro in Henderson's coat. They show them to the young man who tells them to back off. He doesn't take the cigarettes but roars at Henderson and Risto to leave.

CUT TO:

INT. ITN LAND-ROVER, STREETS. DAY.

Risto and Henderson dive into the ITN Land-Rover. Risto is behind the wheel. Henderson looks blank.

HENDERSON

What are we going to do now? Where are we going to go?

Risto has started up the engine. He is full of decision.

RISTO

Mrs Savic. She must keep records. We'll go and talk to her.

HENDERSON

Of course.

Risto drives off.

I should have thought of that.

RISTO

Don't bring her back here, Michael.

HENDERSON

I'm trying not to. That's why I'm here.

RISTO
(*too insistent*)

Promise me.

HENDERSON

Sure.

RISTO

If you say she won't come back when it's over, it makes it possible to believe that it will be over one day.

155

CUT TO:

EXT. ORPHANAGE, SARAJEVO. DAY.

The ITN Land-Rover pulls up. There is no sign of life. Risto gets out first.

CUT TO:

INT. ORPHANAGE. SARAJEVO. DAY.

A soldier is watching from inside the orphanage. He starts to panic. He is only half dressed. He shouts to a friend, another soldier, who isn't dressed at all. The two jump into their clothes and run off out the back door.

CUT TO:

INT. ORPHANAGE, SARAJEVO. DAY.

Meanwhile, Henderson and Risto have come in through the front door. The orphanage is wrecked and deserted. The office drawers are all open and their contents scattered. They jump back at a sudden sound. Then the door behind Henderson opens and he almost dies of fright.

When he looks round, Lucky Strike is there, wearing crude make-up.

> LUCKY STRIKE
> Hello big buddy. Want to do some business? Got cigarettes?

CUT TO:

INT. ORPHANAGE, SARAJEVO. DAY.

Lucky Strike is smoking a cigarette. She inhales deeply, relishing the taste.

> LUCKY STRIKE
> Micky Mouse, Dollar bill, Big Mac, Michael Jackson.

> HENDERSON
> Where is Mrs Savic?

> LUCKY STRIKE
> Many girls trade these for bread but I get how many I want. Enough to smoke, so flip that.

Risto asks her about Mrs Savic in Croatian.

I speak fucking English. Savic fucked off. Totally fucked off.
No one knows where. If you want me to tell you where, it's
going to take you a fucking fortune. I told no one and
everyone wants to know.

HENDERSON
Who wants to know?

LUCKY STRIKE
She was a fucking Serb. Did you know it? She was fucking
nice to me though.

HENDERSON
If you know where she is, it's important.

LUCKY STRIKE
Everyone's looking for Savic. Fuck it. Let's do the business.

HENDERSON
Who's looking for her? Why?

LUCKY STRIKE
The government. They want to lock her up, man. She's a
fucking murderer.

HENDERSON
What?! What's she talking about?

Risto asks her to explain.

LUCKY STRIKE
Two babies were killed in a convoy. It was Savic that put
them on the coach. So now it's Savic who is going to pay.

HENDERSON
She's lying. She's got to be lying.

RISTO
I don't think she is.

LUCKY STRIKE
I like your phone. Give it to me. Then I sell phone time
instead of sex. I get fucking more money.

157

HENDERSON

It doesn't make any sense.

LUCKY STRIKE

Sense? What is sense?

CUT TO:

EXT. ORPHANAGE, SARAJEVO. DAY.

Henderson and Risto making the scary dash back to their ITN Land-Rover. The distant sound of small-arms fire. They jump into the Land-Rover.

CUT TO:

INT./EXT. ITN LAND-ROVER, ORPHANAGE. DAY.

Risto tries to start the Land-Rover up. Nothing. Tries again. Nothing.

RISTO

Shit.

HENDERSON

What? What's going on?

RISTO

The petrol. Someone has stolen the petrol.

The scary desolation opens up around them.

Henderson starts poking at the phone, trying desperately to get through to Jane but without luck. He throws it aside. They look at each other. They get out of the car.

CUT TO:

EXT. ORPHANAGE, SARAJEVO. DAY.

Henderson has locked the car. He starts to walk but Risto calls him back. He is holding up the flak jacket to Henderson. Henderson hesitates.

He takes it and they start to walk, keeping close to the walls.

CUT TO:

158

EXT. STREETS, SARAJEVO. DAY.

Pick up on Risto and Henderson making their way carefully along an empty street. Risto becomes aware that a car is following them.

RISTO

There's a car following us.

HENDERSON

Are you sure?

RISTO

Come on.

They hurry. It keeps coming. They duck down a side street.

CUT TO:

EXT. SIDE STREET, SARAJEVO. DAY.

The car follows. They dive into a doorway and try to get through the door. It's locked and now the car has stopped and the door is opening. They turn to face the danger. A man gets out. He speaks to them.

ZELJKO

Mr Henderson?

Henderson stares. He doesn't really recognize the man. He is well dressed, self-confident, magisterial even.

ZELJKO

You don't recall me. But I recall you. I was waiter in the Holiday Inn. You gave me cigarettes. Can I be of assistance?

A look of bewildered relief passes over the faces of Henderson and Risto.

CUT TO:

EXT. ORPHANAGE, SARAJEVO. DAY.

Risto and Henderson back at their Land-Rover, which Zeljko is filling with petrol from a can.

ZELJKO

You must call me. Petrol is not a problem. And this woman – I am sure I can find her for you. But you must have gifts for her.

159

HENDERSON
I've got cigarettes.

ZELJKO
You must come with me.

CUT TO:

INT. WAREHOUSE, SARAJEVO. DAY.

Zeljko, Risto and Henderson are in a warehouse, stacked with food and domestic goods. Zeljko is moving elegantly along the shelves, placing various goodies in a small cardboard box. Henderson is amazed but Risto is entranced, transported.

HENDERSON
What is this place?

ZELJKO
I help distribute aid. The United Nations needs the help of people on the ground. People like myself.

HENDERSON
But . . . if you distribute it, why is it here? Why isn't it distributed?

ZELJKO
They want to stockpile. In case there is a catastrophe.

HENDERSON
Isn't it a catastrophe now?

ZELJKO
(*smile*)
They believe it will get worse perhaps.

Pick up on Risto. He is letting his finger drift sensually over bags of flour, sugar, jars of molasses. His eyes fill up with tears. Zeljko comes up behind him.

Please. Take some.

RISTO
No. After the siege.

160

I'll reserve some for you.

He puts some chocolate aside, and writes a little label, RISTO – AFTER THE SIEGE.

CUT TO:

EXT. RISTO'S FLAT. NIGHT.

Risto – carrying his gun – lets himself back into his flat. He leaves the light on and the door open for a moment. There is a muttered curse and he reappears in the doorway still with his gun. Another muttered curse and he goes back inside with the gun. Reappears without the gun and sidles along the outside wall, looking for a place to pee. Finds the ideal spot. Sighs contentedly, gets shot by an unseen gunman.

CUT TO:

EXT. RISTO'S FLAT. MORNING.

The ITN Land-Rover pulls up. Henderson and Jane get out, looking fairly leisurely.

HENDERSON

Where is he?

(*calling*)

Risto!

He looks down the back of the alley.

He walks down the alley, past bags of rubbish, and sees something that looks like rubbish. His foot brushes against it and an arm falls out. It is the body of Risto.

Risto! Oh, sweet Jesus, Risto. Jane! Down here! Get help!

Jane comes running and looks down at the body. She gives a big, shuddering sob.

CUT TO:

EXT. BURIAL GROUND, SARAJEVO. DAY.

Henderson and Flynn stand back from the grave.

Jane is at the graveside.

> FLYNN
>
> They've been kind of seeing each other since just after you left.

> HENDERSON
>
> I didn't know.

Henderson looks around, realizing something for the first time.

> FLYNN
>
> I sometimes feel that I'll never get home. That it's not really a place, that it's some kind of disease you've caught.

The camera pulls out and we can see the size of the burial ground.

Henderson, Jane and Flynn walk across it.

> JANE
>
> Will you find the mother?

> HENDERSON
>
> Zeljko says he's found her.

> JANE
>
> Zeljko is a gangster.

> HENDERSON
>
> That's right. At least he has no trouble with checkpoints.

CUT TO:

INT. ZELJKO'S CAR, STREETS/CHECKPOINT. DAY.

Henderson is in the passenger seat as they approach a checkpoint. The militiaman on the checkpoint stands back when he sees the driver. Zeljko smiles graciously.

CUT TO:

EXT. DERELICT FLATS, SARAJEVO. DAY.

Zeljko and Henderson walk confidently through the rubble. Zeljko calls him. He says something in Croatian and points upwards.

CUT TO:

EXT. FLATS, SARAJEVO. DAY.

The door is battered. The windows are polythene.

ZELJKO
Here.

Henderson goes to knock but instead places his hand on the wood and waits.

Zeljko knocks for him.

HENDERSON
Thanks.

CUT TO:

EXT. FLATS, SARAJEVO. DAY.

A young woman answers the door. Henderson scans her face, offers her his hand.

HENDERSON
Mrs Mihaljic?

The young woman shakes her head and starts to talk. Henderson is anxious and distracted.

ZELJKO
This is not her but she lives here. Two families live here now.

Henderson is led into the flat by the young woman.

CUT TO:

INT. MILICIA'S FLAT, SARAJEVO. DAY.

The flat is filthy and overcrowded.

A door is opened, Henderson is waved in. An older woman sits behind the table with a young woman. The woman looks at Henderson. This is Milicia. The young woman's name is Sanja. There is a deck of tarot cards spread out on the table in front of them. Henderson takes a breath.

HENDERSON

She looks like her.

MILICIA

Hen-der-son.

Henderson nods. Milicia looks haunted. Zeljko hands over the box of goodies. Milicia doesn't react. Some of the people in the house look around the door. Milicia shouts at them and they all go away, then starts talking as if to herself.

ZELJKO

She already knows you coming. It's in the cards.

HENDERSON

Then she knows why I am here.

Milicia carries on talking. Sanja translates for her.

SANJA
(*translating Milicia*)

First of all she wishes to thank you for what you have done for Emira . . .

Henderson shifts uncomfortably. Milicia continues.

She says she misses her daughter. She knows she has not been a good mother. In the war she has lost many people. Now she has only Emira left. She is alone. She wants to see her daughter.

HENDERSON

Well that's all very well, but the fact is that Emira is very happy where she is. Before she was just parked up in an orphanage and . . .

SANJA
(*cuts him short*)

I not translate this.

HENDERSON

What?!

SANJA

You must listen.

165

HENDERSON
No. I have listened and . . .

He looks at Zeljko for back-up but Zeljko just gestures to him to be quiet. By now Milicia is talking and Sanja is translating again.

SANJA
She knows she is a bad mother. She knows Emira is more happy with you. But because she is a bad mother she has no memories. She needs some memories. She wants to speak with her daughter. She wants to hear her voice.

Henderson is relieved and moved.

HENDERSON
Yes. Yes of course.

CUT TO:

EXT. STREET, NEAR TV CENTRE, SARAJEVO. DAY.

Zeljko's car pauses at the end of Sniper's Alley. Milicia and Sanja are inside. Zeljko slams his foot down on the accelerator. Milicia and Sanja look green as the car hurtles towards the TV Centre. They hold on to anything they can.

CUT TO:

INT. TV CENTRE, SARAJEVO. DAY.

Henderson leading Milicia and Sanja into the centre. Jane greets them with upraised eyebrows.

HENDERSON
They want to use the satphone.

Henderson puts his hand on Milicia's and takes her to the phone.

CUT TO:

INT. HENDERSON'S HOUSE, ENGLAND. DAY.

The phone rings. Helen picks it up casually. Then freezes.

HELEN

It's your mother. Your mother wants to speak to you.

She turns to face Emira, who is eating a healthy supper and who doesn't react. Helen holds out the phone to her. Emira takes the phone and then leans her head into Helen's body, holding Helen's hand with her free hand.

We can hear Bosnian down the phone. Emira listens intently for a while.

EMIRA

I want Michael. Michael?

CUT TO:

INT. TV CENTRE, SARAJEVO. DAY.

Henderson on the phone in Sarajevo. Milicia listens to her daughter's voice as she speaks to Henderson. Big tears well up in her eyes.

Milicia starts to cry. She says something to Zeljko.

ZELJKO

She cannot understand. She cannot understand what her daughter is saying.

Henderson takes the phone.

HENDERSON

Emira? You've got to speak Bosnian. It's your mother.

Henderson hands back the phone and starts to root in his bag. He finds a video and puts it on. It shows Emira happily playing in a London garden. Milicia watches, transfixed.

EMIRA
(*over phone*)

Hello? I'm happy. Thank you.

Milicia gets tearful. She says something to Sanja. Sanja translates.

SANJA

She will sign.

167

HENDERSON
Oh. Yes. I mean, thank you.

He looks for the documents while Milicia keeps watching the video.

CUT TO:

INT. ZELJKO'S CAR, SARAJEVO STREETS. DAY.

Zeljko and Henderson drive through the streets of Sarajevo. Henderson catches sight of the Altar Boy disappearing down a side street.

HENDERSON
Stop the car.

Zeljko pulls over.

There is someone I have to see.

ZELJKO
Good luck.

HENDERSON
Goodbye.

They shake hands. Henderson gets out of the car. Zeljko watches him go and then drives off.

CUT TO:

EXT. SARAJEVO STREETS (CONTINUOUS). DAY.

There are lots of people walking in this road, all walking the same way. The Altar Boy disappears into the crowd. Henderson starts to walk more quickly.

The crowd gets thicker. He can hear distant cello music. He glimpses the Altar Boy and keeps walking after him. The crowd keeps growing and moving.

CUT TO:

EXT. SQUARE. SARAJEVO (CONTINUOUS). DAY.

Suddenly Henderson is in a square and there, up on the rostrum, Jacket, the cellist, is playing his cello. He stands with the crowd as the music

rises over the ruins. Henderson sees Lucky Strike in the crowd. He edges over to her and gives her his mobile phone. On the other side of the dias, he sees the Altar Boy staring up at Jacket, lost in the ecstasy of music.

Before the credits roll, captions give us the latest details on Sarajevo – the death toll, how many children killed, how many days the siege has lasted, etc.